Table of Contents

CHAPTER 1: MAKING PROFIT ON THE FIRST DEAL 3

CHAPTER 2: LIFTING A PAINTBRUSH-NEVER 13

CHAPTER 3: REHAB BY FINDING PROPERTIES 31

CHAPTER 4: FINDING PROPERTIES USING A STAMP 54

CHAPTER 5: EVALUATION DEALING PROCESS USING THE THREE-STEP REHAB 79

CHAPTER 6: FINANCING REHABS .. 90

CHAPTER 7: PROPERTIES ESTIMATION FOR REPAIRS 109

CHAPTER 8: REHAB MANAGEMENT *130*

CHAPTER 9: CREATION OF COMPREHENSIVE WORK SCOPE....140

CHAPTER 10: RECRUITING PERFECT CONTRACTOR......................155

CHAPTER 11: CONTRACT CLOSEOUT AND FINAL PAYMENT.......................181

CHAPTER 12: THE SELLING SYSTEM 198

CHAPTER 13: POSTGAME ANALYSIS 235

CHAPTER 14: COMMON SELLING BUSINESS...263

CHAPTER 15: A SYSTEM FOR KEEPING AND GROWING BUSINESS 276

CONCLUSION.......................287

CHAPTER 1: MAKING PROFIT ON THE FIRST DEAL

You may believe that you need a ton of cash to break into the land business — yet that couldn't possibly be more off-base. Neither earlier learning nor a financial balance loaded with money is a necessity. Indeed, you can exploit more chances in the event that you have both experience and cash. In the expressions of one of my mentors, "Each ace was at one time a calamity." No one realizes what they're doing well toward the start. However, we as a whole begin someplace.

The Obstacle

The greatest obstacle you will probably confront is fear. Individuals are reluctant to come up short, to be ill-equipped, that it'll be excessively troublesome, that they won't have enough cash. A few people even fear achievement. These are for the most part authentic concerns, yet the manner in which you handle this fear will manage your future as a private redeveloper. Most individuals consider fear to be a stop sign—however, it's a focus sign. That twinge of stress in the pit of your stomach is a sign to focus on what you don't have the foggiest idea, what you have to know, and what you are as of now acquainted with. Consider an open door that you realized you needed to take, yet didn't. What kept you down? By what method will that be diverse this time around? When you change your view of fear, you will see innumerable chances. All the more critically, you'll invest your time and vitality all the more profitable. Rather than maintaining a strategic distance from fear, you should greet fear wholeheartedly. When you recognize fear, at that point you have quite recently distinguished what you have to realize and accumulate more data to push ahead with certainty. You don't need to know every one of the appropriate responses; you simply need to get to and be happy to approach the individuals who do. The general populations you encircle yourself with are fundamental to your prosperity as a financial specialist.

The Opportunity

Have you at any point been driving or strolling someplace and see a property that required some adoration? You know—the one with a front garden taller than your abdomen or that needs an outside paint occupation and siding more than you need a hairstyle.

Our first legend to disperse is that you can make a benefit on any house. You can just make a benefit on the correct house—the one that needs work, has an issue to be tackled and has a proprietor who is propelled for you to make a success win to get it. When you locate the correct house, you would then be able to actualize the seven-organize recovery framework without lifting a paintbrush. In each market—up or down, purchasers or vendors—there is dependably somebody disclosing to you that presently is certainly not a decent time to put resources into land. Ask yourself the accompanying three inquiries when you hear that guidance:

1. Does this individual cause multiple times more than I do monetarily?

2. Does this individual have the way of life and the opportunity of time that I want?

3. Is this individual even experienced and as of now profiting in the land?

Ninety-nine percent of the time the response to these three inquiries will be no. Everybody has a supposition. In the event that I tuned in to everybody who disclosed to me that presently isn't the correct time to get into the land, I would, in any case, be at my first occupation.

Start Thinking Like An Investor

Each dimension of salary you want requests an alternate adaptation of you. On the other hand, you approach recovery as a do-it-without anyone else's help diversion, you'll see that in your arrival. Your time isn't best spent painting the house yourself to set aside some cash. This is a device that averts many would-be speculators from really getting to the following dimension. The following dimension is the point at which you invest less energy in one arrangement, make more benefit on that bargain, and invest your time in things that could easily compare to land. My brilliant standard on rehabbing land is, "Never get your hands grimy." Our main responsibility is to discover roused bargains, fund-raise, and deal with an effective recovery. You are in the matter of turning cash. How rapidly would you be able to put one dollar in so you can get three dollars out?

At the point when this turns out to be second nature to you, you will understand that rehabbing is a vehicle for duplicating your dollars. When you set aside some cash by taking every necessary step yourself, you are hindering the activity, putting out inferior work, and botching different chances while you are taking a shot at the site. Fundamentally, by getting your hands messy, you hinder the chance to recover your cash sooner. At last, your responsibility is to put one dollar out of your pocket as a financial specialist and perceive how rapidly and proficiently you can bring two dollars back in your pocket. Put your contractual workers in an effective framework; this shows regard for their time and capacity. Clarify that you are not an errand kid or young lady to bring materials for the house. You should have enough trust in yourself to genuinely comprehend where your time is best spent—and the accompanying parts of this book will indicate you simply that.

CHAPTER 2: LIFTING A PAINTBRUSH-NEVER

Envision what might occur if everybody you knew, paying little heed to their calling, did their very own duties—with no assistance from a CPA or bookkeeper. Give me a chance to give you a precedent. Your interests and gifts lie somewhere else, however you need to designate 6 to 12 hours of your time documenting your expenses or more. Truly, you may spare a minimal expenditure, yet you are relinquishing something that is progressively significant—and you aren't working at your most noteworthy nor utilizing your time. As we talked about in the past section, a recovery financial specialist ought not to be performing take a shot at the house. Or maybe, you should concentrate on exercises that will make you, your temporary workers, and your whole group more cash: discovering bargains, financing bargains, fixing bargains, and flipping bargains. Focusing on these high-need errands will decidedly affect everybody engaged with these undertakings.

The Wrongdoers

When you get your first rehab bargain, you will be excited to the point that you may overlook how significant your time is as an investor. For the principal month, you will drive companions, family, and colleagues to your new rehab venture without acknowledging how much time you are squandering. You disregard to thoroughly consider things, get ready, or recognize the contractual workers and work that need to occur. Before you understand it, you'll have consumed a month and innumerable visits to the house by not being readied and sorted out with a framework. In money-related terms, you simply paid for a month of holding a cost. After advance installments, service charges, taxes, insurance, and upkeep you don't have anything to appear for all that you have done so far. When you at long last settle on a couple of choices, you hurriedly employ a contractual worker. Tragically, you neglected to talk with, prescreen, and check the contractual worker's referrals; and you didn't set up the best possible working relationship through the six basic archives. What's more, you contracted your companions, moms, sisters, and children. The contractual worker begins the activity with a simple to use the extent of work, which means you strolled them around the house while pointing with your forefinger and verbally disclosing to them what you need to be done in each room. You don't record anything, not to mention significantly consider having them sign the six basic reports that will keep them inside the guidelines, course of events, and spending important for you to succeed.

At last, the activity begins. Be that as it may, the temporary workers require 50 percent of the settled upon cost as an upfront installment before they'll begin working. So you pay them. Since the main influence you have over any contractual worker is the cash you have not yet paid them, you're stuck in an unfortunate situation. What motivator do they need to complete the work on your course of events or hit your achievements since they as of now have half of the undertaking cash in their pocket?

As the rehab begins, you are anxious to take an interest and get your hands messy. You continue to ask the temporary worker what you can help with, at which time he gives you a rundown of provisions to get from Lowe's or Home Depot. While you may think you are helping, you simply transformed yourself into a $10/hour errand kid/young lady.

The activity achieves around 25 percent finishing and the contractual worker clarifies that he kept running into some unforeseen expenses and work that he needs more cash for. Keep in mind, you effectively paid 50 percent of the temporary worker's expense in advance and they have just finished 25 percent of the work. Presently they are requesting more cash and you pay them another 30 percent of the expense to continue working. You're getting yourself into a significant gap here.

The temporary worker returns to work and quickly finishes another 10 percent of the task. Their quick advancement enables you to like your choice. In any case, the temporary worker happens to secure another position and customer that is happy to pay them another 50 percent upfront installment. He takes on the extra customer and gets 50 percent of the cash and now has a commitment to another person's task. Meanwhile, nobody is working at your home. Developing concerned, you call the temporary worker who gives you one reason after another with respect to why they are not at the undertaking site, and guarantees to be at your property the following day.

In any case, they are by and by absent the next day—after you've ceaselessly called and left various phone messages. You presently have a house that is 35 percent complete in the wake of having paid out 80 percent of the expense of the activity. You have a temporary worker that never again answers your telephone calls and sends you straight to voice message. Of course, for what reason would they answer your calls? They as of now have a 45 percent net revenue (80 percent of the installment less 35 percent of work finished) while never setting foot in your home again.

Start Thinking Like Business Owner

A consumer centers on what things cost; an entrepreneur centers around what things are worth and the esteem they can bring into their lives. A shopper doesn't burn through cash they don't have. An entrepreneur spends other individuals' cash on whatever will take an incentive back to their business and life by using influence. A buyer is incapacitated with fear of assigning work that won't turn out in the same class as they can do it. An entrepreneur can hardly wait to appoint and have somebody carry out the responsibility superior to anything they did as such they can concentrate on developing different territories of their business.

Ninety-nine percent of us are modified to trust that time is cash. This is essentially false. Would you be able to give me a case of when you had the option to spend your cash to get additional time back in your life? When did the cash you procure enable you to return and purchase time so you could go through it with a friend or family member who is never again here? Shockingly, none of us can give a case of when cash purchased time. This is on the grounds that time isn't cash—the time is everything! There is one dimension playing field for the rich and poor, the wealthy and those who lack wealth, the special and the unprivileged: We all work with a similar 24 hours in multi-day. The separating factor between individuals is the means by which they utilize their opportunity to figure out what they achieve and accomplish. You should likewise reconsider your meaning of influence. Fruitful private redeveloper influences everything. They influence cash by setting up, getting to, or discovering credit to acquire reserves and further their business. They influence mentors, specialists, counselors, and data to diminish their expectation to absorb information. They influence authorized and protected proficient temporary workers to enable them to finish an astounding rehab.

An MWA is the lowest pay permitted by law movement. MWAs are employments you ought to re-appropriate and expel from your day by day plan as your time turns out to be increasingly significant so you don't stall out as a professional in your very own business. As a hopeful land investor, making fruitful propensities is basic to attempt right off the bat in your profession. A few alternatives may be to employ a cleaning administration for your home or pay the $12–$20 charge to have the supermarket convey perishables you request on the web. There are innumerable approaches to give others a chance to finish the humble errands we as a whole need to finish in our lives, with the goal that you can save your opportunity to focus on moneymaking exercises. Whenever you are finishing an errand, inquire as to whether you can contact support to make additional time and get your next $25,000 benefit bargain.

A private redeveloper is a more trustworthy title than a flipper or a rehabber or simply some houseman. A private redeveloper redesigns the blemishes in a given neighborhood and produces quality lodging that everybody can be pleased with. A private redeveloper makes occupations inside their locale. A private redeveloper is somebody who invests wholeheartedly in their work, their locale, and makes a social effect on each house with character and uprightness. It doesn't make a difference in the event that you need to consider this as a low maintenance attempt to make the infrequent rehab benefit or on the off chance that you need to go fulltime and increment your profit potential past anything you have ever envisioned. Being a private redeveloper is about the attitude, working more brilliant and not harder, utilizing your time, and conveying the best item (a completed rehab) the correct way (pulling grants and following all code consistency), and conveying a home to families that will deal with it for quite a long time to come.

Time is everything. Try not to succumb to the do-it-without anyone's help attitude. Begin having a similar outlook as an entrepreneur beginning today. Influence cash, assets, frameworks, guides, and whatever else that is accessible to get you to your own and money related objectives. Through embracing this outlook and disposition you will rise above from the specialist in your own business to a genuine business visionary who appreciates the advantage of owning a business, instead of most experts who have a business that possesses them.

CHAPTER 3: REHAB BY FINDING PROPERTIES

Any entrepreneur realizes that on the off chance that you can't or don't have the foggiest idea how to advertise, you won't be ready to go for long. What's more, discovering executioner rehab bargains has an inseparable tie to showcasing. A decent arrangement is focused on the chance to which we can include an incentive as an investor. In the following couple of parts, I'm going to impart to you some suitable on the web, disconnected, and arrange to promote methodologies to discover bargains.

So what is the key to getting a decent arrangement? It starts with finding an aroused dealer. In the event that a vender's home does not require fixes, on the off chance that they have no timetable to sell, or in the event that they don't have squeezing circumstance to unravel monetarily or by and by, they don't have to pitch their home to a rehabber. Keep in mind, on the off chance that you can't increase the value of the circumstance as a rehab purchaser, at that point you can't make a success win. Making an idea on a house in flawless condition and recorded on the Multiple Listing Service (MLS) for as much as possible isn't the manner by which we make an incentive as a rehab investor. You should continually showcase for arrangements to purchase, cash to raise, temporary workers to work with, and dealers to pitch to. Therefore, organize advertising is the primary methodology we depict, as it requires no direct cash to begin. System promoting is an amazingly savvy and proactive type of advertising, constrained uniquely by your eagerness to move your feet and your mouth to cooperate with the general population around you. The general objective of system advertising is to advance your business and instruct the majority on how you might be of administration to them, or the other way around. You are setting up these connections so that those with whom your system can profit by your item, administrations, and business openings. These connections can prompt extra business, either straightforwardly or in a roundabout way through a referral.

There are instruments that can enable you to deal with the majority of the connections your structure. A client relationship director program, also called a CRM, can enable you to sort out your contacts and computerize your capacity to stay in contact with them. This innovation quickening agent enables investors to keep up working compatibility with the majority of their contacts and leads. Like such a significant number of others, the land is eventually a business based upon connections—explicitly, as far as what number of associations you can make and be readied when your next circumstance presents itself. The more you present yourself as a land proficient who can purchase and sell properties, acquire cash and secure it against genuine property, or contract and pay temporary workers, the more system advertising referrals will come your way after some time.

The Power of Networking

One of the extraordinary parts of working in real estate is that everybody, sooner or later, will require a spot to lease or purchase. You ought to experience no difficulty starting a discussion and discovering shared conviction; everybody needs a spot to call home. What's more, as a real estate investor, everybody is presently a potential customer and client!

The way to fruitful systems administration is to perceive incredible open doors when they present themselves. It is safe to say that you are exploiting organizing openings in your regular daily existence? It tends to be barely noticeable out on the ones you accept that aren't significant to your business. Be that as it may, any network where you have manufactured notoriety gives a chance to organize. Indeed, even individuals from a non–real estate related network or gathering of which is a piece of knowledge and your hard-working attitude in excess of an investor or more interesting that you just met. This sort of chance is exceptional to your hunt, as you have officially invested energy fabricating and made common regard with these network individuals. Keep in mind, since you are in the business of real estate, everybody will require your administration sooner or later, so told them about the open door you have. The majority of your contacts are an important advantage for your real estate business. What's more, you will locate that numerous individuals are really searching for the open doors that your business can give.

As a rehab investor, there are a few people who you ought to always be organizing with and coordinating your advertising endeavors toward. You will need to adjust yourself to individuals who have made progress out and about what you are currently voyaging. A great deal of your systems administration will include discovering people who have been the place you need to go—and the individuals who can help get you to arrive. You should enroll the assistance of a few experienced people for your group to develop and work proficiently. Every individual you come into contact with while working together turns into a piece of that group. For example, the achievement of your contractual worker is legitimately related to the accomplishment of your redesign business. Everything streams down and everybody must depend on the group.

Working with Other Investors

Numerous investors really get their chance by collaborating with different investors and taking the arrangements that they may not need or can't get financing for. A rendition of this is wholesaling. There are two unique kinds of investors out there: tenderfoot investors and propelled investors. You need to connect with both. New investors should seize the opportunity to band together with different investors. Fledglings in real estate regularly discover bargains that they need help with collecting. I've experienced endless novices who required training on the most proficient method to structure an arrangement, or who don't have enough money to support it. The two gatherings associated with such a coordinated effort make a success win by including esteem and building up a long haul relationship to push ahead with. Regardless of whether it's information, capital, or essentially time and exertion that you can focus on a task, you generally need to carry something to the table to expand the likelihood of them working with you.

You will likewise need and need to collaborate with fruitful real estate investors who have experienced everything. On the off chance that a prepared investor has an excessive number of arrangements in their pipeline or a greater undertaking that requests their consideration, you might almost certainly buy their next property; consequently, they get a discount benefit. Many experienced investors are eager to accomplice and offer ability or subsidizing. It's essential to exercise alert when engaging the possibility of an association. You have to deliberately consider any joint effort you make. You ought to refrain from collaborating with somebody with whom you don't have a long-standing relationship. The best methodology is to pitch an arrangement to or purchase an arrangement from somebody so each gathering can go for broke and control their very own fate with no debates. You likewise need to ensure the numbers work when acquiring property from a distributor. Any great distributor will dependably leave enough benefit for the rehabber. The way to building an association with different investors is to enhance their business through execution or learning shared.

Systems administration with great home loan dealers is basic to your rehab business; they are a fundamental piece of your group who can assist you with your financing needs. All the more significantly, a great home loan intermediary can give you referrals for good arrangements to purchase, and furthermore allude potential purchasers who are not yet working with a home loan proficient. Home loan representatives are likewise important for promoting accomplices. Since they aren't legitimately contending with you for an arrangement, they can supplement your promoting endeavors—and you can part the expenses. For instance, you can convey a post office based mail piece with photos of your homes to sell on one side and data in regards to the home loan agents' business on the other. This enables potential purchasers to see the house that is available to be purchased and ask about any financing they may require. A customary authorized home loan specialist can't pay you a referral expense for sending them business, yet they can part advertising expenses with you on your next battle to discover purchasers or dealers.

As a private redeveloper, you'll have to add real estate specialists to your group. They can give a strong wellspring of leads for purchasing and selling homes. Numerous investors reject the idea of working with a specialist when they get their very own operator permit and do the work themselves. Regardless of whether you do get your real estate permit, you should recollect that you are as a matter of first importance an investor, not a Realtor. I don't have my permit, so I depend on generally excellent, investor-disapproved of real estate specialists to work with.

Acquiring your very own permit isn't important. I have effectively finished many exchanges regardless of not having mine. The key is to search out, distinguish, and select real estate operators who will all the while assemble your business. There are numerous operators who will get in touch with you even before they list a property on the off chance that they realize you are a genuine player in the business.

You need to oblige specialists' needs as much as they are taking into account yours. You will likely turn into their go-to contact—an expert in your general vicinity of redesigning properties. Tell Realtors you are not scared of homes that need work and remodels. Working with investors offers specialists the chance to realize rehash business and various commissions. Operators have the chance to execute various arrangements a year with your help. By going about as a double operator in an exchange, speaking to both the purchaser and the vendor, they acquire the two sides of the commission. A specialist will come to consider you to be an entirely profitable contact with whom they will strive to keep. Telling great Realtors that you will possibly give them the posting of any rehab property they convey to you is a gigantic advantage and a route for an investor to get paid on a similar house twice.

Regardless of whether they are abandonment, probate, ousting, or separation lawyers, these people are probably the most notable individuals with whom you can organize. Consider what number of potential dealers, loan specialists, and purchasers they experience amid their day by day course of business. These power players come into contact with customers who are regularly needing arranging a property or might be in a circumstance where they are genuinely inspired to sell—particularly on the off chance that they're experiencing a situational inspiration, for example, a separation. Also, lawyers will have data about properties in abandonment and the individuals who are experiencing probate. Also, we should not disregard the other significant motivation to coordinate with lawyers: cash. Lawyers are an incredible wellspring of private assets. Regardless of whether not loaning themselves, they know and encourage exchanges for private moneylenders. I committed the error from the get-go in my vocation of neglecting to talk about potential financing openings with my lawyer, who had officially finalized many negotiations at the time. I no doubt passed up a few opportunities to distinguish another loaning source as a result of my inability to perceive my lawyer as a wellspring of financing.

CHAPTER 4: FINDING PROPERTIES USING A STAMP

Direct mail marketing

Direct postal mail is a standout amongst the most dominant and demonstrated advertising devices today. It is likewise a standout amongst the most economical and effective approaches to produce leads for your real estate business. To discover beneficial arrangements on a predictable premise, it's basic to use immediate, coordinated advertising, as it can grant you openings that other rehab promoting techniques frequently disregard. Standard mail is such an integral asset since it is quantifiable. You can follow reactions and measure your ROI (rate of return) effortlessly. In contrast to publicizing, it's additionally discernible, cheap, and gives results that are substantial. When building up your rehab promoting the plan, it's critical to make a practical framework that can anticipate the number of leads coming into your pipeline every month. This part gives you the apparatuses important to make a fruitful advertising effort. I've executed this demonstrated framework in my own business, yielding productive rehab bargains. 40% of your prosperity is connected to whom you explicitly target. There are a few kinds of records that investors use to finish this assignment that we can separate into two classifications: critical and not all that dire. The dire classification rundown incorporates mortgage holders who are into a greater extent a race to sell their homes, potentially on the grounds that they are confronting a course of events or misfortune. These incorporate pre-abandonment records,

30/60/90-day-late records, chapter 11 records, fire harmed and code infringement records, and duty lien records. Note that an enormous part of the leads from dire records will be time-touchy. So the prior you achieve these customers, the better. The not really dire class comprises of property holders who should not sell their home, however, they are as yet roused. These are acquired property records, non-attendant/out-of-state mortgage holder records, probate records, lapsed postings, and without a worry in the world records. Be that as it may, remember that in spite of the fact that the not really pressing rundown might not have a basic need to sell, they can finish up turning into a portion of your most beneficial arrangements. Much like the pressing mailing records, timing is essential; no one can really tell when the dealer might be prepared. Hence, finishing a multi-letter trickle crusade is significant.

What sort of advertising pieces would you say you are utilizing for your mailings? The manner in which you approach somebody can affect their reaction. I would say, prospects on the dire rundown react better to an expert mailing on organization letterhead. The mortgage holders' credit and business are regularly in question, so they need to feel like they are working with an accomplished proficient. Then again, not really dire mortgage holders are frequently bound to react to an individual touch. Now and again, mailing them a less expert looking yellow letter is regularly more successful than a postcard or letter on organization letterhead. How would you convey your post office based mail? There are two different ways: you can satisfy yourself, or influence and pay a satisfaction organization. Clearly, gathering your rundown in-house will be more practical, yet you will more than likely just have the option to deal with satisfying a few mailing records at once, as it is very tedious. Be that as it may, in the event that you redistribute your crusade to a satisfaction organization, it is robotized for you. While your costs will be higher, you never again have the pressure and dissatisfaction of satisfaction. When you re-appropriate, you're likewise ready to actualize various battles.

Sending Messages Consistently

Consistency is fundamental with regards to regular postal mail advertising. When you have adequately actualized your methodology, it's pivotal to send your post office based mail battles at customary interims. When you have everything set up, you can follow each battle's adequacy. One of the greatest errors real estate investors makes is conveying only a couple of mailings and after that quitting. They are called battles which areas it should be. You have to actualize them three to multiple times before you can decide if they're working to support you. In the event that you have gone to the cost of acquiring a prospect list or invested the energy to order one, you deserve to debilitate all conceivable outcomes before surrendering. It is endlessly better and financially more brilliant to send a letter or postcard multiple times to 1,000 individuals than to send one letter to 5,000 prospects.

Determining budget and plan

Deciding a spending limit for your regular postal mail battles is vital to your real estate contributing business. What is reproducible and realistic spending that you can use each and every week? In spite of the fact that you might not have an answer at first, you will need to make a couple of reaction rates and spending presumptions to decide a rough quantifiable profit in advance. This will enable you to assess whether your promoting effort costs are advocated. It might be out of your usual range of familiarity to burn through cash that you can't promptly substantiate, however it's tied in with defining an objective and focusing on the procedure. The most ideal approach to arrange your post office based mail crusades is to set them up at the same time and order them by date. Tuesdays are the greatest days for mail to touch base, as it is typically the lightest mail day of the week. Your mailings are bound to emerge with less challenge, so time them carefully.

Identifying the target market and obtaining lists

Characterizing your objective market is tied in with picking your crowd and sourcing the rundown to which you will mail. Before you even start composing, it's essential that you comprehend your intended interest group.

Your promoting message ought to mirror the goals of those with whom you are trying to associate. For instance, in the event that you are concentrating on single-family homes in pre-dispossession, your message should exclude data about purchasing charge lien abandonments. Superfluous data can twist your expected message. You need your prospects to feel as if you comprehend their own circumstance. Every individual bit of your post office based mail crusade ought to talk legitimately to its peruser.

Keep in mind, every single one of these rundowns you can bring esteem and make a success win to assemble an arrangement. On the off chance that you can't make a success win, you ought to never push ahead with an arrangement. All things considered, you can join a portion of the prospects on these rundowns and send them similar mailers. For instance, 30/60/multi day records can be joined with pre-NOD. Furthermore, fire-harmed property leads can be joined with the code authorization infringement list. For whatever length of time that the objective rundown and informing are harmonious, you can circulate a similar mailer.

Setting Marketing Campaign

A postcard is a basically structured mailing piece with your fundamental data that lets merchants quickly know how they can profit by functioning with you. You ought to use the little space effectively to energize the merchant and to get them to see how you can cure their circumstance. Postcards are economical, surrender the message front, and don't require stamps or envelope stuffing. Ensure that you incorporate a convincing feature, data about how you will take care of the mortgage holder's concern, and your contact data.

A yellow letter should utilize penmanship or a textual style that imitates penmanship on yellow legitimate or note pad paper, and be fixed in a written by hand envelope. This showcasing piece is intended to be as peaceable as could be expected under the circumstances; it should look to the merchant as though it were originating from a companion. Yellow letters have an incredible reaction rate; they are likely a standout amongst the best mailers to use.

Your feature is the absolute most significant thing at the highest point of your letter or on the facade of your postcard or envelope. You should ask yourself when you take a gander at your mail piece, "What grabs my eye?" If your answer isn't the feature, make a few changes. Your feature ought to be clear, snappy, and striking, and should grab the eye of mortgage holders who have empty properties or a noteworthy remaining task at hand to improve their property. Solid articulations provoke interest and intrigue and brief a merchant to call, email, or go to your crush page site.

Setting up the inbound system

Before you even consider conveying a post office based mail piece, you should choose how you're going to deal with reactions. You need your lead consumption frameworks set up before conveying any mailings. It is safe to say that you are going to accept the telephone brings in your office? Is it accurate to say that you are going to utilize a call focus? Or on the other hand, would you say you will send your prospects to your site to submit data to you that goes into your database?

Fulfilling campaigns

Numerous investors begin by satisfying their battles themselves, particularly initially. This methodology may set aside you some quick cash, however, you will more than likely have the option to deal with just a few mailing records at once. A ton of investors become effectively overpowered with the time that in-house satisfaction requires, so they, in the long run, choose to redistribute their crusades to an outside mail-satisfaction organization. Utilizing a satisfaction organization gives a turnkey answer for sending your mass mailings to people in general. Despite the fact that it will cost more, you kill the pressure and dissatisfaction of satisfaction, and it's simpler to actualize various crusades. An option in contrast to utilizing an expert mail house is to procure somebody to deal with your battles in-house. Commonly, littler mailings, for example, lapsed postings, charge lien, and probate records—are a lot simpler to satisfy yourself.

A portion of the bigger records, for example, pre-abandonments, acquired properties, out of state proprietors, and non-attendant proprietors will more than likely require a mail house to satisfy.

Tracking Mail and Stay Organized

Following and assessing your post office based mail crusades viably will enable you to figure out where your cash is best spent. The exact opposite thing you need to do is invest cash and energy in a post office based mail battle that did not deliver any leads that transformed into arrangements. Test and measure your advertising on a week after week and month to month premise, so you can make the fundamental acclimations to create results.

In the event that you don't grow post office based mail frameworks, you'll have no compelling method for guaranteeing that you achieve your planned vendors every single week. Setting up these frameworks enables your battles to keep running on autopilot—and enables you to concentrate your endeavors on gathering with dealers to purchase properties. Ensure there is a method for following the reaction rate for each bit of post office based mail you convey. This is the best way to decide if it's working as it should. Without the legitimate following, it will be hard to spend your advertising dollars shrewdly. This will improve your reaction rate and increment your introduction, along these lines enabling you to settle on savvy choices with your showcasing dollars.

You generally need to follow your outcomes dependent on the objectives you set for your promoting crusade. For instance, in the event that you needed to build traffic to your site or become the number of inbound calls, set up components that enable you to decide whether web traffic or calls expanded and by how much. On the off chance that you needed more home seller drives, what number of home sellers leads were created? Following your outcomes begins with one exceptionally straightforward inquiry: "How could you find out about us?" You should pose this inquiry at each connection (inbound call takers, web shapes, and so forth.). I'd likewise prescribe including an interesting reaction following framework (i.e., a site presentation page for that particular post office based mail piece or a special without toll number, and so on.). Post office based mail advertising is a standout amongst the most practical showcasing methods we can apply as private redevelopers searching for our next circumstance and arrangement. It is focused on the advertising approach and can be extremely successful for testing and attempting diverse promoting efforts. Send more than one letter to a potential purchaser, mail frequently, and development. Regular postal mail is a focused on and compelling type of promoting to execute and locate your next rehab bargain.

CHAPTER 5: EVALUATION DEALING PROCESS USING THE THREE-STEP REHAB

Phone Analysis

Before you can assess a rehab bargain, you must have a lead—that is, an imminent merchant. This happens while you are on the telephone with an imminent merchant or real estate operator. Finding a lead and after that utilizing a framework to bring down and compose the Seller's data is basic.

This initial phase in the arrangement assessment procedure expects you to pose an assortment of intentional inquiries to measure the dealer's inspiration. For instance, you'll have to ask concerning whether the property is in dilapidation or needing any updates to make it attractive and reasonable. Some of the time an individual who has lived in a home for a considerable length of time won't realize it needs real fixes and will erroneously advise you that no fixes or updates are required. In cases like these, you are in a split second back at the starting point.

Desktop analysis

In the event that you got agreeable solutions to your inquiries amid Step 1 and have chosen that the subject property has potential, you're prepared for Step 2. This should occur after the underlying telephone call with the merchant, yet before your in-person meeting. This is the biggest piece of the arrangement examination and will decide if you visit the subject property. This is likewise when you'll find that 80 to 85 percent of the leads that come in are not hot leads, and will require extra follow-up to make them arrangement commendable. The rest of the 15 to 20 percent of your leads will more than likely be hot leads. For them, you should dissect the money related numbers and make bundles of practically identical offers of like-type properties (otherwise called comparables or comps) and purchasing arrangement envelopes.

There are five basic money-related regions to comprehend so as to investigate the quantities of your potential arrangement. At the point when done effectively, this will let you know correctly whether you should push ahead with this property. The main piece you won't have precise now is the evaluated rehab since regardless you have to visit and physically walk through the subject property. In any case, you can get a harsh thought of the improvement cost through your telephone addressing and investigation. These are the five budgetary territories to which you should give close consideration when evaluating the result or expenses of your potential arrangement. Our training understudies influence our arrangement analyzer programming, which enables them to connect three numbers and releases an answer in a moment or two. With training and mindfulness, you will improve each time you examine an arrangement by the numbers.

Before you begin inquiring about practically identical offers of like-type properties you should affirm the data the merchant, specialist, or outsider gave you about the property by pulling a property card. You can discover this snippet of data for practically any property in the province records where the property is found. These are regularly accessible online in many states and contain insights regarding the property including deal value history, proprietorship history, surveyed esteem (for assessment purposes), the warmed area, the number of rooms and washrooms, and significantly more. This is a decent spot to search for any irregularities between what the dealer let you know and the official expense records. Try not to be reluctant to get back to the merchant and check data preceding gathering if need be. The Multiple Listing Service to which real estate specialists approach is an incredible device for social affair data for your arrangement examination. The MLS will disclose to you the number of rooms and restrooms, area, the business value, normal days available, data on the territory the property is found, and significantly more.

In-person Analysis

This phase of the arrangement assessment procedure begins 30 to 45 minutes before your gathering with the merchant, and it reaches out to your in-person meeting in his or her home. Amid this stage, you will play out a revaluation in transit to your gathering. You'll at that point walk the property and check whether it matches up to the merchant's depiction while you decide progressively precise esteem. Over the span of your gathering, it's basic you accept the open door to manufacture affinity and trust with the dealer. When you've finished all your drive-by examinations, ensure you re-breakdown your as-is esteem. It's critical to check for irregularities with the subject property and the encompassing homes. This is an ideal opportunity to ensure your leave system is as yet the best choice—after you've seen the encompassing territory.

The gathering with a vendor is an energizing occasion since you just never recognize what you're going to discover when you get to the property. You may find that the property needs unquestionably more work than the dealer let on, or you get the lovely amazement of finding that you have a real jewel that you'll have the option to exit with insignificant fixes. The reason for the purchasing arrangement is to manufacture compatibility with the vendor.

Holding fast to a framework to survey, dissect, and assess your arrangements encourages your spare time and get more arrangements. Do as much homework and investigation before you get to the dealer meeting so you are arranged and can deal with any inquiries or protests the potential merchant may raise. The arrangement is the key in examining and getting more rehab bargains.

CHAPTER 6: FINANCING REHABS

Leveraging systems and funding people's money

The greatest obstruction numerous real estate investors face when beginning with their first rehab is their powerlessness to acquire financing for in excess of a bunch of arrangements at one time. Home loan loaning limitations can make things troublesome and keep investors from extending their real estate venture portfolios. So as to benefit from the absolute best and most productive gives, you should comprehend your financing choices. Financing is the thing that causes the real estate world to go round. Besides getting quality training, gaining admittance to capital for your arrangements it of most extreme significance to you as a private redeveloper. Subsidizing enables you to make an influence. To be effective, you should probably buy properties with generally little measures of your own cash. The inquiry won't be about how to use when you're the first beginning; all the more squeezing issue is finding the cash to subsidize your first arrangement and get your business off the ground. The best part is: it doesn't need to be your very own cash. As you figure out how to fund-raise, you can obtain a large number of dollars for your arrangements. Numerous new investors are soothed to find that you can get this cash paying little respect to your present financing standings or FICO assessment.

Development capital is the key. Your interest in this book is a case of development capital. By taking the exercises contained in these pages, you will pick up information on the most proficient method to begin and fund-raise for your exchange capital, which enables you to purchase your next rehab. When you sell that first rehab, you can utilize a portion of that cash to support your next showcasing effort and other operational expenses. The key is to dependably put as a matter of first importance into development capital; this is the place you'll get the assets and information to handle the other two capital prerequisites inside your business.

Funding deals with private money

It didn't take long for my accomplices and me to realize we expected to accomplish more arrangements. We required better access to capital, so we needed to make associations with moneylenders.

Building up these vital connections gave us the certainty to make more offers and accomplish more arrangements. Also, approaching extra assets protected us from a ton of hazard by giving our business greater liquidity. Private loan specialists can be just about any individual who is eager to hear you out and has the cash to loan. As a rule, you will make private moneylenders by really showing individuals how to make more than the half-percent return they are as of now procuring in their investment account.

Building money saves throughout the years likewise caused us to realize that private loaning is a phenomenal method to gain a high rate of come back from our rehab benefits. Rather than simply letting the cash we earned from flips sit in the bank or purchasing our next property with the money, we've found an approach to really loan our cash for higher rates of return. We realize that it is so basic to have obligation finance for other authorize investors to loan their cash nearby our very own for a decent hazard balanced current return through Grand Coast Capital Group.

There are individuals out there with cash who need to put resources into something verified by a real resource. You get the opportunity to offer them the chance to put their cash in the real estate you need to purchase. Private moneylenders can carry speed and proficiency to your exchanges. Moreover, you will have a lot more prominent influence when you buy a property utilizing private-money reserves. Huge numbers of the properties obtained by investors need a deal to occur inside 10 to 14 days. Customary banks expect 30 to 45 days to close credit and won't loan on rehab bargains that are not bearable, in this manner making numerous traditional home deals drop out of the agreement because of financing. Having the option to utilize money permits you a much lower price tag, and diminishes your general hazard.

Using Private Money

Private loan specialists support will be basically assigned to the price tag and remodel cost. In the end, the moneylender will get a home loan on the home alongside a promissory note. You will at that point approach your ordinary remodel process. Numerous banks will loan at a level of the after-fix esteem (assessed deals cost upon finished rehab), normally 70 to 80 percent.

Notwithstanding the promissory note and home loan/trust deed, you will include the private loan specialist to your property protection as a misfortune payee. Along these lines, in the event that anything happens to the house, the insurance agency will pay back the advance before they give you any cash. This is essential to comprehend, as it lessens the loan specialist's hazard when the correct controls are set up. When you complete the redesign stage, you rundown and sell the property. When you can close on the property with a purchaser, the moneylender gets its guidelines in addition to premium installment. You need to ensure this procedure runs easily, particularly with private moneylenders. When you've been fruitful in doing your first arrangement with a private moneylender, it's critical to construct a long haul, commonly gainful relationship so the loan specialist will hold returning to you.

Fund Dealing by Private Lenders

Most private moneylenders use money held in many sorts of financial balances. These can be gotten to rapidly and can subsidize your arrangements in minutes, rather than hours or days. Charges are commonly negligible for wire exchanges and clerk's checks. These can be financial records, investment accounts, or currency market accounts. Home value credit extension is an extremely ground-breaking wellspring of financing that numerous individuals have and don't consider. Unleveraged value is dead cash that isn't making any premium, and that you can without much of a stretch tap into. It's an approach to ensure you're in the first position when we're prepared to pull the trigger on a property.

Anybody with great credit and a steady salary can get these individual advances and mark credit extensions from most banks or credit associations. An ever-increasing number of private moneylenders are utilizing their IRA assets to put resources into real estate. A self-coordinated IRA is basically equivalent to a customary IRA, however, it enables you to buy a more extensive scope of ventures, including real estate. A great many people don't realize they can change caretakers and put their cash into real estate notes and exchanges.

Ventures are an approach to give your investment funds something to do acquiring more cash. Be that as it may, if your stocks and ventures have not executed as you had expected, it may be a great opportunity to think about different speculations. As you probably are aware, you can sell stocks when you wish. Here and there you need the cash to buy real estate. Discovering private cash isn't so troublesome as individuals might suspect. While numerous individuals may not be effectively hoping to contribute, they have cash lounging around and might be available to contributing with you on the off chance that you simply inquire. All things considered, at the present time it's simply lounging around not procuring interest.

We've discovered that having a private cash believability parcel for your business can be a profitable showcasing piece when you are talking with a conceivable private moneylender. You have to demonstrate yourself to be a commendable investor when you first begin. This bundle ought to incorporate a little data about you, how the organization was established, and even your experience and training. You should exhibit your insight, aptitude, and even affability on the off chance that you anticipate that outsiders should depend on their cash to you.

Utilize web-based life, online journals, and a site to fabricate your marking and believability. Having an expert private loaning aide will awe any bank. Notwithstanding private cash, you have to assemble an association with a hard money lender.

This is the most significant cash relationship you will make to move your business forward, much more so than with private loan specialists. Hard money lenders are composed of semi-institutional loan specialists who ought to be authorized to loan cash to investors and rehabbers purchasing properties needing fixes. They give present moment, high-rate advances with expenses that enable a real estate investor to buy rehab to extend rapidly and effectively. As a rule, these are bargains that investors probably won't most likely buy generally through conventional moneylenders. Dissimilar to customary bank advances, hard moneylenders offer momentary advances, and will likewise normally loan cash for the expenses of development on a rehab property. This segment of financing is appropriated in draws against work being done, and assets for rehab are normally set up on an installment timetable of work that has been finished. This is fundamentally the same as the installment plan you would make for contractual workers for your rehab venture. Draws and installments are paid after work is finished.

The name "hard cash" does not suggest that these advances are hard to obtain; truth be told, it's really the inverse. While the terms and criteria for hard-cash credits require more data, they are frequently simpler and more solid than some other banks. Hard moneylenders base their endorsement on the arrangement and the home first, and afterward, they survey you actually. This implies you may, in reality, fit the bill for a hard-cash advance with terrible credit, a pending abandonment, or pay that is hard to demonstrate on the off chance that you have a lot. The magnificence of hard moneylenders is they comprehend the business: they center around the arrangement, not the individual hoping to make it.

CHAPTER 7: PROPERTIES ESTIMATION FOR REPAIRS

Capable rehabbers must sharpen their aptitudes for evaluating fixes on properties. Much progressively significant is to classify what is required and what isn't in an opportune and effective way on your first physical walkthrough. At last, your objective ought to be to gauge fixes in an hour or less while at the house, and figure out what completely should be fixed or remodeled to accomplish the after-fix esteem (ARV), sell the property, and catch the benefit toward the back.

Evaluating fixes rapidly enables you to address questions and appropriately handle any complaints you may experience. In the event that you can't address a merchant's inquiries regarding how much work is required on the house you are purchasing and to what extent you gauge the rehab to take, you'll begin to lose the energy and certainty for completing the arrangement. Responding to the redesign addresses your potential merchant solicits limitlessly expands your odds from securing your next arrangement.

Taking longer than 30 minutes to gauge fixes is likely an exercise in futility and vitality. A decent arrangement endures 24 hours, best case scenario. In the event that you can't decide an arrangement inside that time period, another person will—and you will finish up missing out. You will probably go through just 20 minutes to an hour and get inside a couple of thousand dollars of the genuine fixes. We definitely realize that creation offers is the way toward support into our securing cost. So we should comprehend what value the house will sell for once it is repaired, less the benefit potential and less the rehab cost.

Rooftop is one noteworthy region of the house that most new investors appear to get off-base. As a rule, they gauge it erroneously in light of dread or straightforward powerlessness to comprehend the assessed expense to fix or supplant a rooftop. To begin, roofers gauge a material occupation by what number of squares the rooftop needs. A square for rooftops is a 10 × 10 region or 100 square feet.

Drains can have a tremendous long haul sway on a home's life span. A great many people don't realize that on most houses, awful establishments, sodden cellars, and water issues regularly begin from terrible water the board. Canals help catch and push water far from the house. The majority of this makes it imperative to recognize canals as a fix or not for you as a private redeveloper. Including canals and diverting water far from the house will begin the procedure in taking care of establishment issues and water issues.

Supplanting or painting the siding or stucco is an incredible chance to really change a house's appearance. You can supplant, fix, or simply paint the current material. Siding in numerous territories is likewise an admissible type of embodiment for toxic paint. What an astounding supernatural occurrence a layer of paint can be to any blemish! Paint is absolutely one of those home upgrades that can enable any house to go from rubbish to money. Painting an outside and inside is a cost that pays for itself in spades.

Fixing a carport is normally a venture of simply wiping and whiting it out. You are commonly best served to simply factor in a fix cost that would cover a basic get out, fix, and another layer of white paint. The main time I would propose generally would be in the event that you are assessing fixes on a top of the line property or if the carport is a huge selling highlight. In the event that the property has an isolates carport that is essentially falling over, you may much think about decimating it. You will need to take a gander at the benefit of having a withdrawn carport before remaking. It may not bode well in numerous regions of the nation to modify a withdrew carport if the house is in a lower-end region. In these situations, the ongoing deals and comparables ought to decide if you reconstruct the structure or relinquish it.

Affirm whether different houses that are selling in the region have carports. Provided that this is true, what is the value differential between the houses that do and don't have carports? When you have this data, you'll have to contrast that with the expense of revamping the carport. For instance, if every one of the deals and practically identical houses with carports are selling for $20,000 more than normal, and your carport needs a total revamp that will cost $10,000, at that point you should push ahead with structure the carport. Be that as it may, if the expense for revamping the carport is $20,000 and the expanded deal cost is $20,000, at that point you have some further contemplations. On the off chance that your property will sell sooner or it is the thing that somebody needs to see to make an idea on your property at that value, at that point you have to take a gander at the work and cost as an element expected to exchange and sell the house rapidly. Regardless of whether the expense of modifying the carport was $20,000 and it just included $20,000 of esteem, you would in any case need to reconstruct the carport as your deals and comparable are demonstrating that it will be difficult to sell the subject property at your evaluated ARV without a carport.

Arranging has such a sensational impact on how your home shows, its control request, and the enthusiastic effect on potential purchasers. The best thing is it very well may be truly moderate and, contingent upon what should be done, most employments take just 10 to 12 hours to finish. It's astounding what some mulch, new shrubs, and laying some new grass or turf can do to the presence of the front of your home.

In certain business sectors, houses are recorded and sold without machines. In any case, you ought to dependably spending plan for another refrigerator, stove, and dishwasher—this dependably demonstrates the house well and gets it sold quicker. Completing a kitchen or house rehab and leaving old or utilized machines is simply not savvy. In the meantime, you would prefer not to put incredibly highquality apparatuses in an area that does not require them to get the house sold. Be savvy. Supplant old apparatuses with new ones that match or beat the challenge presently available to be purchased at your value point and in your neighborhood. In the present aggressive market of machines, treated steel apparatuses have turned out to be entirely moderate. All things considered: I generally propose purchasing and putting in new apparatuses as opposed to keeping and reusing old or existing machines.

Some contend that restrooms could really compare to kitchens when appearing and selling a house. A few purchasers will buy a house since it has a Jacuzzi tub or an extravagant downpour showerhead. Most restrooms can be pulled separated and set up back together at a genuinely minimal effort.

In any case, you don't need such a large number of various materials separating the basic territories when rehabbing a little house, since it will make the house feel much littler. For instance, in the event that you have a little kitchen beside the lounge area and you place hardwood in the lounge area and tile in the kitchen, at that point these two materials will complement the break and how little the two spaces really are; in this manner contracting the space by making it feel littler. When you're managing littler spaces, keep the material the equivalent between abutting rooms. This is a territory where most new investors get apprehensive on the grounds that they ordinarily don't have involvement with this establishment, the cost required, or the material required. A property's mechanical fixes can represent the moment of truth the achievement of a rehab venture. Planning appropriately and evaluating these fixes or potential substitutions will eventually put you as a rehab purchaser in the best position to finalize negotiations. These parts are at last what keep purchasers from purchasing a house, particularly in the event that they don't turn new or upward to-date with a long, valuable life in front of them. We generally need to assess these distinctive mechanicals in the house with a sharp eye and an exact manner of thinking. As examined before in the section, you should likewise apply the "pay now or pay later" idea for mechanicals. This is one of the regions of the house that will either frighten off potential purchasers or offers, or they will just make an idea with a fix credit or solicitation on your completed rehab.

This is a significant piece of each house and rehab. Our fix gauge sheet is intended to spending plan the pipes to incorporate both the kitchen and the restroom plumbing. Evident pipes fixes will be the issues that are not working. Optional pipes can be something like improving the channel lines in the kitchen from a few creeps for better long haul waste and utilization. In chilly climate expresses, your handyman frequently assumes a double job of pipes and warming establishment. Numerous handymen can chip away at warming frameworks, for example, high temp water baseboard warming units, just as their pipes skill. This is great to know; it can help spare expense and time on your activity and enable you to consult with one tradesman for both pipes and warming.

Lighting is one of the enhancements that can have a colossal enthusiastic effect well beyond its expense to introduce. Adding lights to a room, the kitchen, scene, and outside can totally upgrade the mind-set and feel. Low-voltage lighting with dimmers is likewise an extraordinary touch to help show and sell houses. Recessed lighting all through is a pleasant selling highlight and overhaul. Much the same as pipes, the electrical numbers on the fix sheet incorporate the kitchen lighting and washroom lighting. Warming, ventilation, and cooling (HVAC) is the innovation of blowing sight-seeing through sheet metal or pipes to warm a house. The concentration here is to dependably have a tidy or forward-thinking framework. On the off chance that you don't, at that point you have to spending plan for it.

A standout amongst the most significant things for you to pass on and set up as a private redeveloper is that you are genius licenses. We will examine this more in future parts, however rehab investors who don't force grants will in the long run either lose business or be criticized as an investor who compromises. Pulling grants is an important piece of guaranteeing that your business flourishes, improves neighborhoods and, obviously, is gainful. As expert private redevelopers, we generally work with our structure divisions and have authorized and proficient contractual workers who force the best possible grants for each activity. License expenses change crosswise over regions, since construction standards and expenses differ radically relying upon what part of the nation you live in. This is the reason it's basic to acquaint yourself with the procedure and expenses for pulling and paying for grants.

CHAPTER 8: REHAB MANAGEMENT

The Seven-Stage Rehab System is the way to my rehabbing equation. I have made and improved a seven-arrange procedure of the critical advances that should be overseen and executed with the goal that I or anybody in my group can have accomplishment from the very first moment overseeing and actualizing a rehab. Whenever pursued, this framework will enable you to spare time by working with the best contractual workers, utilizing the right desk work and understandings to control the timetable, spending plan, and nature of the completed item. The net consequence of following the Seven-Stage Rehab System in Part II is an effectively finished rehab that you will invest heavily in as you rundown and market it available to be purchased.

Measuring Everything

The most significant activities in becoming your rehab business are getting the hang of, comprehension, and acing the whole rehab procedure and framework—which implies that you won't invest the majority of your energy in the jobsite. All through the procedure, you will likewise begin to create associations with temporary workers and subcontractors. Great contractual workers are the most basic colleagues for structure and developing your private redevelopment business.

Readiness is the way to remain on calendar and inside spending plan for a rehab. You have to build up a reasonable thought of what remodels and upgrades you need to embrace before including a contractual worker. You ought to likewise have an unmistakable thought of your financial limit with the goal that you can build up a realistic extent of work.

Rehab Preparation

This will be your first visit to the property once you really claim the arrangement. The objective is, in one visit, to assemble all the data and vital subtleties to assemble the extent of work that will be utilized to offer and contract temporary workers to take the necessary steps. A standout amongst your most significant errands to finish amid this first walkthrough after you close on the property is to recognize the things you have to fix, just as the things that will help sell the house when complete. For instance, would it be advisable for you to expel a nonload-bearing divider between the kitchen and lounge room or add a window to exploit a decent view? Would it be advisable for you to add a lookout window to add splendor to a dull room? These are only an example of the choices that currently should be concluded before you begin the rehab with your distinguished temporary worker group—not in the center or after.

Walkthrough Property

Separate your walkthrough into similar segments that you will use for your extent of work dependent on the property fix gauge sheet: outside, inside, and mechanicals. This will keep the walkthrough methodical and keep you from disregarding regions that need consideration.

Begin by moving toward the home's outside as a potential purchaser would. Notice everything that gives you a negative impression. Awful finishing, stripping paint, and haggard fencing are only a portion of the things that can mood killer intrigued purchasers before they ever stroll in the entryway. Additionally search for things, for example, an open air seating territory or new turf that can be added to build the home's estimation. Ensure every outside light work and test programmed carport entryway openers and water system frameworks on the off chance that they are available. Start the procedure again on the house's inside. Focus on the main thing you notice and feel when you stroll in the home. How might you improve an awful impression or upgrade a decent impression? Experience each room and observe everything about to get a precise thought of precisely how much work should be completed a second time with the property fix gauge sheet, yet with a lot more noteworthy detail. You will require this data when setting up your extent of work. Measure and sketch territories of the property where you might need to change the format, for example, the washrooms or kitchens, and incorporate a particular issue zones. Note the area of mechanical framework things, for example, the water warmer and the heater. Stage 1 of the Seven-Stage Rehab System is your first visit to the subject house after you have shut on it. You would prefer not to take various excursions to assemble this data. On the off chance that you do take numerous outings, you are sitting around idly, and we have built up that for private redevelopers, time is… everything! Amid this stage you are adding to the refinements of your unique property fix gauge sheet and searching for all different subtleties that should be tended to or improved. Presently we should get the chance to arrange 2 and begin the extent of work back at the home office.

CHAPTER 9: CREATION OF COMPREHENSIVE WORK SCOPE

The extent of work, or the SOW, fills in as the establishment of your rehab. It's an understanding among you and your temporary worker that frameworks the definite subtleties of the task and materials you are mentioning the contractual workers to execute—a point by point plan for the day. A SOW limits miscommunications among gatherings and considers the temporary worker responsible to the settled upon terms and precisely what you need and need done.

For instance, suppose that you've chosen to modernize the kitchen, fix up the restrooms, and re-try the floors. While you may have an unmistakable thought of what those three things involve, it would be unimaginable for a temporary worker to offer the work dependent on that scope—considerably less really complete any work that you would favor. Your concept of another kitchen redesign and a contractual worker's concept of another kitchen can be two radically results. When you don't have a composed SOW, you risk getting the kitchen the contractual worker needs and not what you need. This is the place contentions and liquefies downs happen among temporary workers and investors. Try not to fall into this snare. Continuously complete a SOW before you procure and enlist a temporary worker.

The best similarity for a SOW is "an extent of work is to a rehab as a screenplay is to a film." You have to illuminate everything about—to paint shading, spigot installation, kitchen cupboards, apparatuses, and substantially more. Without a plainly characterized and well thought-out SOW, it is exceptionally simple for task expenses to winding crazy and breaks your financial limit. Building up a point by point SOW is your most significant assignment as the private redeveloper. When the activity begins, you ought to be out searching for the following arrangement and fund-raising for future venture exercises—not regulating work at your rehab. The SOW shields you from being an on location venture director and enables you to be a genuine private redeveloper. Your most astounding and best use is discovering bargains, fund-raising, and settling on abnormal state advancement choices… not minding the jobsite to ensure work completes. The SOW framework gets you more cash-flow and makes the expert contractual workers you procure glad; it enables the temporary workers to do what they specialize in and keeps you out of their hair.

Developing Scope of Work

To begin on your SOW, you start with the property fix gauge sheet you finished while auditing the advanced pictures you took nearby on your first visit to settle on official conclusions on the things that should be finished.

When you have an unpleasant SOW that is inside your spending limit, revisit and include more detail. This is the point at which you choose what modernizing the kitchen implies explicitly: Are you going to take it full scale and begin without any preparation, or basically supplant reap gold apparatuses with hardened steel and update the cupboard equipment? You'll clearly need to fix whatever is broken, however you might almost certainly rescue things for reuse. Be as exhaustive and point by point as conceivable when building up your SOW. One of the significant reasons for going over spending plan or getting behind timetable in a development undertaking is an absence of appropriate arranging, definition, and detail at the venture's start. You should be definitive and have an unmistakable vision of what you need the finished result to resemble. On the off chance that you don't have the foggiest idea what you need, it's absolutely impossible your contractual worker can have accomplishment with you and your venture.

Example of Kitchen

We should survey the framework that my organization and instructing understudies use and influence to help them effectively assembled the detail of upgrades utilizing a kitchen remodel. In our extent of work we need to explicitly choose and distinguish the precise completing material with thing numbers and SKU numbers that the contractual worker will buy and introducing. By demonstrating the contractual worker that we know the material costs, this keeps them genuine and prevents them from increasing material expenses so they can make extra benefits.

This precedent and outline are to demonstrate to you the subtleties of the framework that will get you the ideal results you need as long as you take every necessary step before the temporary workers set foot in your home. This should commute home the point that the most work we will do on the rehab is at the extent of-work organize. This is the place we settle on all the abnormal state choices as a private redeveloper.

When you've amassed your offered bundle, you should print at any rate 10 duplicates to leave at the projet site. You at that point drive to the house for the second time after you have shut on and possess the property to drop them off. When you experience the contractual worker prescreening process, you'll send potential temporary workers to the site with the lockbox code to get an offer bundle and inspect the property for offering. Illuminate them regarding the due date for their statement so you can survey and grant the triumphant offer to begin work. This procedure spares you a long stretch of time of time that would somehow or another be spent driving, holding up at houses, and strolling numerous temporary workers through the activity. When we talk about rehabbing properties without lifting a paintbrush, you can see it is tied in with utilizing a framework and esteeming your time at each progression of the procedure.

Double-checking scope of work

One of the greatest concerns when completing a rehab is keeping the home's post-redesign an incentive in accordance with the comparables in the area. Before you begin thinking about the majority of the work you need to do to the house, take a gander at later practically identical deals in the territory to ensure they are in accordance with the value you need to exchange it for. For instance, suppose you obtained a property for $130,000; you might want to place $30,000 in redesigns into it, and exchange for $190,000. Nonetheless, later equivalent deals in that area are averaging $160,000. In light of your redesign sum, your business cost would put you $30,000 over the comparables in the zone. Despite the fact that you made the house look fabulous, you would experience considerable difficulties offering it for $30,000 more than different homes in the zone. In addition to the fact that purchasers would favor the more affordable houses, they would likewise experience issues getting an advance for more than the evaluated estimation of the home, which is to a great extent dictated by deals comparables. Utilize your extent of work as an apparatus to characterize the venture and ensure that the new after-fix esteem remains inside sensible breaking points. Keep the comparables you use to get an underlying ballpark figure and keep on refreshing comparables all through the undertaking. Toward the finish of the undertaking, you will have an exceptional parcel that, alongside the extent of work, your potential purchasers can present to their bank to help the price tag. The extent of work is the place you settle on all the official choices on precisely what you need to go into your completed rehab. It is the most significant stage for setting up your rehab on a fruitful stage and expanding the accomplishment of any contractual worker you contract to convey the completed item you need. You should remain centered and recognize the subtleties in the extent of work—your temporary workers and future benefits will thank you for it.

CHAPTER 10: RECRUITING PERFECT CONTRACTOR

When you have settled your extent of work and set up together your offer bundle, you are prepared to meeting and welcome temporary workers the chance to offer on the task. The accomplishment of your rehabs will rely upon two things: having a decent, strong framework set up like the Seven-Stage Rehab System, and employing a quality contractual worker to work inside that framework. So as to draw in these sorts of temporary workers, you need to offer them on the open doors that you give. You can do this by utilizing a temporary worker lift pitch as first experience with another contractual worker, regardless of whether face to face, through a report, for example, a contractual worker validity bundle, or via telephone. You should plan your lift contribute with a particular result mind.

As referenced above, you will need to set up a temporary worker validity parcel to advertise for contractual workers. This is particularly significant on the off chance that you are welcoming contractual workers who are new to you or your association to offer on your task. Your contractual worker believability bundle isn't work explicit—so once you have one created, it will just need minor refreshing every once in a while. Since your ultimate objective is to set up a confiding in association with your contractual worker, you will need to put some exertion into making an expert looking report. A temporary worker believability parcel format is accessible for the majority of our instructing understudies and enables them to get straight down to business.

Potential temporary workers might be worried about whether you will probably acquire predictable work. Once more, you are inspiring your temporary worker to build up a decent working relationship—so you should set up trust by spreading out how you regard contractual workers and manage them reasonably. Tell your potential temporary workers that you are an investor with a proceeding with stream of work for them on the off chance that you can get great estimating. An example extent of work will give your potential temporary workers a smart thought of what kind of customer you will be to work with. A composed SOW normally implies a sorted out customer.

Your past undertakings talk obviously about the measures you set for your temporary workers, and will give potential contractual workers a superior comprehension of your quality desires. On the off chance that you are new, you have to reference the mentor or putting network wherein you enlisted to become familiar with their framework and influence the experience as you begin.

Tell your potential contractual workers what attributes and characteristics you are searching for in a contracting association. Propel your temporary worker by referencing the high potential for rehash business on the off chance that they pursue your measures. Tell them that they can create a quality item and redesign on schedule and on spending plan. You additionally need to detail any permitting, protection, and guarantee prerequisites you have—which may serve to promptly wipe out certain temporary workers. You can incorporate an example temporary worker understanding, pay plan, etc to indicate potential contractual workers that you mean business and are a legitimate investor or firm.

Finding Quality Contractors

Promoting for temporary workers is critical—so significant, truth be told, that I have a explicit promoting framework and prescreening process (counting a full application and meet) that we use before working with them. Keep in mind: 50 percent of the accomplishment of your rehab is subject to the contractual workers you find and contract. So finding a quality temporary worker requires somewhat more exertion than simply looking in the Yellow Pages. Basically, a quality temporary worker is proficient, capable, authorized, and guaranteed. They will have the most noteworthy likelihood to work inside your framework and do the best, most effective, work conceivable.

There are a few sites with temporary worker databases that you can look. I've recorded a couple underneath that I've been effective with. In spite of the fact that each of the four locales expect you to enroll to look for temporary workers, Angie's List is the one in particular that charges a yearly expense to utilize its administrations. It additionally changes dependent on the zone you are looking. Offer Clerk works somewhat better from the other three destinations, acting increasingly like a commercial center where you, as the proprietor, can post a vocation for contractual workers to offer on.

First off, if a temporary worker is notable at a supply store, that implies they have rehash work. On the off chance that they have rehash work, that implies they are fulfilling clients and doing great quality work, else they would not keep on landing more positions. Lastly, if the supply-store staff part eludes them, they pay their bills and are regularly monetarily dependable.

These are extraordinary spots to meet a great deal of temporary workers and system with the group and staff at the experts' work area. Ensure on the off chance that you are really going to meet and search for temporary workers at these stores that you arrive early in light of the fact that that is the point at which the great contractual workers invest energy at Lowe's or Home Depot—not amidst the day when they ought to work and finishing occupations.

Your nearby structure division sees a ton of temporary workers and can be an incredible asset whenever taken care of accurately. Discovering contractual workers along these lines guarantees that you are managing people who know about the allowing procedure and that they really draw licenses, do quality work, and know the nearby overseers.

Since the structure office is a metropolitan division, they won't almost certainly show inclination for one temporary worker over another. At the end of the day, they can't suggest a temporary worker for you. You should just go in to present yourself and disclose to them that you are endeavoring to discover neighborhood temporary workers to take a shot at your undertakings that are authorized and safeguarded. Tell the structure office that you will recognize empty and broken down houses that you plan on reviving and returning on the expense moves to support the city and acquire charge income (this is the means by which they get paid). This gives them an opening to share the contractual workers they work with all the time without appearing.

Disclose to contractual workers how your framework for finishing rehabs will free them up to do what they specialize in and shield them from carrying out their responsibility and yours. Tell them that you are an investor and will have a constant flow of ventures for the correct contractual worker, so they won't need to stress over where the following employment is originating from. Make it unmistakable, also, that you pay instantly and eagerly for finished work. You likewise need to set aside the effort to pitch your organization standards. Right now is an ideal opportunity to clarify your zero-resistance approach for low quality work or absence of demonstrable skill. Set desires front and center. Tell the temporary workers that you trust that great remodels originate from great contractual workers. Ensure you accentuate how basic tuning in and correspondence are to the task's prosperity, and cultivate cooperation among all gatherings included.

There are sure criteria you should discover in a temporary worker to guarantee a positive encounter. The accompanying inquiries help center what you ought to look and talking for when you meet and prescreen temporary workers.

You additionally need to ensure that your potential contractual worker isn't extended excessively flimsy. On the off chance that you discover that the material temporary worker you're talking with as of now has three representatives and three material occupations in the meantime, you should need to reevaluate. You needn't bother with long periods of rehabbing knowledge to reveal to you that somebody with that numerous occupations and that couple of specialists will more than likely be moderate, lethargic, and worried.

In our framework, it is significant that we contract straightforwardly and pay all contractual workers. That implies the craftsman, handyman, circuit tester, HVAC, etc. What we are attempting to maintain a strategic distance from is paying one individual the majority of our cash who at that point requests that somebody do work at your home who never gets paid. This is the point at which you keep running into the issue of debates and repairman's liens. Nobody thinks increasingly about your cash and your activity more than you. Our self-employed entity understanding spells out that they can't procure any subcontractors without our endorsement.

You would prefer not to work with any temporary worker who isn't authorized and isn't eager to get the best possible licenses. You likewise need to avoid any individual who doesn't have protection, as they will end up being a risk for you. It's unquestionably an additional layer of security for you to pick just the authorized temporary workers who don't compromise. Keep in mind, any harm or wounds that occur on the jobsite will be your concern on the off chance that you are sufficiently imprudent to work with an uninsured contractual worker.

You need a contractual worker who is monetarily steady enough to have the option to front material costs utilizing their supply house credit extensions and isn't constraining you for cash constantly. Contractual workers who need cash all the time are constantly hard to work with. Contractual workers who don't have a demonstrated reputation of taking care of cash and maintaining their business are an obligation and could be a future issue already in the works on the off chance that you employ them.

Clearly a temporary worker won't give you references from clients who were disappointed with their work, yet you will most likely become familiar with a ton about the contractual worker from their past customers. Try not to be hesitant to ask references explicit inquiries about the contractual worker's work propensities, team, and polished skill. Review past employments will give you a solid case of the consideration and quality this individual puts into their undertakings. They can talk the discussion, however in the event that the workmanship is poor, you would prefer not to work with them.

You must have a decent framework so as to encounter an extraordinary temporary worker. Numerous new investors or those without a framework procure great temporary workers; however even the best contractual worker will flop in an awful framework or no framework by any means. The main individual to fault in this circumstance is you, the investor, for not carrying out your responsibility in advance with a definite extent of work. Realize that a decent contractual worker is extremely valuable. Deal with them, develop with them, learn with them, and the two gatherings will profit. The way to our contractual worker framework is prevalent correspondence. The evaluating I have shared hitherto is discount valuing, not retail estimating. Which means on the off chance that you can't impart well that you are an investor who can include esteem, make their activity simple with your demonstrated framework, and potentially give them future work, they will give you one-off retail evaluating. Essentially, on the off chance that you can't sell the temporary worker on the advantages of working with you, at that point it will be difficult for them to perceive any reason why they should give you limited discount evaluating and special treatment over a property holder doing their one-time kitchen redesign.

A significant hint that will set aside you time and cash: before you send a potential temporary worker to offer, give them your evaluated spending plan for the venture. In the event that it's unrealistically low, it's your temporary worker's business to legitimize and instruct you regarding why their statement is higher than the spending you initially accepted. In any case, you should gauge a tad lower than your suitable spending plan on the off chance that you have overestimated in certain regions, and the temporary worker can complete the activity the at a lower cost.

When you have prescreened various qualified, authorized, and protected contractual workers to cite your home, you are in the last leg. These cautiously prescreened contractual workers at that point get the chance to offer on your present undertaking. Ensure you convey to all temporary workers the course of events for sending back the statement separation structure so you can survey all offers and grant the activity.

Assess each offer for polished methodology, exactness, and generally speaking feel. On the off chance that you have any inquiries on a thing that a contractual worker has incorporated into his or her offer, don't delay to request explanation and training. The most minimal offer isn't the programmed answer to whom we work with. When you have pursued the prescreening framework and have a gathering of value contractual workers submitting offers, it is alright to pursue your impulse and gut about who you accept will be the best working accomplice and colleague to begin and finish your rehab.

CHAPTER 11: CONTRACT CLOSEOUT AND FINAL PAYMENT

At the point when the last achievement has been finished on the rehab, you are prepared to begin finishing off the task.

Regardless of how great your contractual worker is, they will definitely miss a couple of subtleties. Before you complete a careful walkthrough of the undertaking with the contractual worker to create punch-list things that should be tended to, have the temporary worker utilize a vocation fruition agenda. This agenda enables the temporary worker to affirm everything is finished and in great working request before you turn out to the house to make the last punch list.

This is additionally frequently alluded to as the last CO (endorsement of inhabitance). This documentation is expected to cut off out and sign on the majority of your pulled structure licenses. You would prefer not to cause the last installment until you to have a duplicate of the last, closed down grants or another type of verification that the structure grant is presently shut with the structure division agreeable to them. Try not to depend on a call to the structure office; in the event that you don't really have something physically marked from the Building Department, this could return to you nibble you.

This is a rundown that you as the proprietor and investor make upon last walkthrough to get little or enormous things that were missed or still should be fixed before you pony up all required funds. You would prefer not to make various outings to the property with your contractual worker to go over definite punch-list things. I suggest buying a move of blue painter's tape and separating any territories all through the home that need finish up work so they don't get missed.

When the licenses have been marked and the punch rundown finished, and you are content with the finished task, have the temporary worker sign the last and unrestricted waiver of lien before issuing the last installment for the activity. This record shows that both you and the temporary worker concur that the undertaking is finished per the agreement, and that the contractual worker does not have any grounds to make a case or document a specialist's lien against the venture. The measure of the last installment ought to be incorporated with the waiver of lien and is recognized as installment in full.

The initial three things should be done before you approve the work and issue the last installment. On the off chance that you don't have physical confirmation that the structure licenses are shut as per the general inclination of the structure authority and office, don't issue the last installment. In the event that regardless you have things on your punch list that are not fixed or finished, don't issue the last installment. On the off chance that the contractual worker has not physically marked the last lien waiver, completely don't issue last installment.

It is critical to finish these last strides in a specific order. Don't, under any conditions, cause the last installment to the contractual worker until you to have gotten the testament of inhabitance from the Building Department upon last walkthrough, and until the temporary worker has finished the last punch list. When those means are finished, the temporary worker signs the last and genuine lien waiver, at which time you may issue the last check and thank the contractual worker for an occupation all around done.

Home Staging

This is the last phase of the rehab procedure before you begin showcasing and selling your completed rehab. Now the property ought to be expertly cleaned and arranged to make it put its best self forward. The most significant outlook you are presently moving toward your completed house with is the eye of a potential purchaser. Take your proprietor cap off and put on the potential-purchaser cap. From the time you dismantle up to the property, is the arranging impeccable? Is the outside house clean and appearing? When you open the front entryway does it stick or open easily? Inside is the house spotless, organized, and appearing? You have put a great deal of work into rehabbing your property, so go the additional mile now and put some exertion into ensuring it is ideal for the primary starting showings so it will sell right away.

Presently isn't an ideal opportunity to get shabby. Nobody will need to purchase a grimy house. The exact opposite thing you need a potential purchaser to be unfavorably influenced by in making an offer is they felt the property was excessively grimy and did not show well. A perfect house rises to a spotless deal!

Arranging your recently finished rehab is a critical detail that could decide the speed of your deal. An unstaged property spends a normal of around multiple times longer available than an expertly organized home. Organizing transforms a customary space into an unprecedented home by featuring it's best highlights. An unfilled house can point out blemishes, which keeps purchasers from having the option to see the home's actual potential.

At the point when the arranging is finished, get an expert photographic artist to take photos of your new rehab. This will enable you to acquaint your purchasers with an assortment of outwardly engaging photos that mirror the house's actual character. It is imperative to incorporate a top notch image of each element you are attempting to sell—individual photographs of the parlor, kitchen, lounge area, family room, main room, terrace, and any extra element worth uncovering. Exhibiting extra resources, for example, area, can help also. Incorporate any perspectives your property may have of the shoreline, a lake, mountains, a fairway, and some other selling point.

Anyway enticing it might be, don't utilize cell phone pictures for your posting just to set aside a little cash. It has been demonstrated over and over that a posting shot with a highquality camera will get a larger number of perspectives and sell for more cash than those with a low-quality simple to use camera. Since such a large number of planned purchasers these days have the advantage of doing their shopping on the web, they will incline toward the properties that show the best photographs while seeing them on the web. When the house has been organized and captured, the outside finishing is right on the money, and the inside cleaning has happened, complete a buyer's-eye walkthrough before you list the house. This implies you have to remove your investor-proprietor cap and adopt the thought process of a purchaser from the moment you dismantle up to the property. Homebuyers are looking for a specific number of rooms, showers, and area. This is just founded on how huge their family is, what number of children they have, and the necessities they require as a purchaser.

The home purchasing choice is significant, so purchasers are exceptionally specific. Frequently they've had their Realtor show them house after house and still can't choose one. They are searching for the ideal house. Our objective with our rehab, arranging, and valuing of the house is to give only that. At the point when your completed, single-family home hits the market with a fresh out of the plastic new kitchen with the tile backsplash—every single new washroom with a hot tub and downpour showerhead—and delightful new hardwood and rug flooring, they realize this is the house for them! Consider it: 90 percent of the houses they have strolled through and seen are not completely redesigned homes. Actually, most are right now being lived in. When they strolled through your opposition, they saw another family's photos on the divider, another kid's blurbs up in the restroom. When they see the washrooms in these lived in houses, they smell like—well, restrooms.

Your posting has proficient photos of your completed rehab. The house itself is immaculate and clean. It is consummately organized and looks astounding. What's more, best of all, your completed rehab is a similar cost as the other lived-in houses. At the point when potential purchasers contrast your home with the others they have seen, and they realize they are in a similar neighborhood, same cost, and same number of rooms and showers—it's an easy decision. This is the brilliant thing about private redevelopment. Single-family homes are the strongest piece of the real estate showcase. Regardless of what the market resembles, individuals are continually getting hitched and searching for their first home. Individuals are continually migrating a result of their work. Individuals are continually becoming out of their present home since they had another kid. On the off chance that your house is rehabbed, evaluated right, and meets the three purchasing criteria, it will effectively turn into another sold rehab home and rehab benefit delivered by the Seven-Stage Rehab System.

CHAPTER 12: THE SELLING SYSTEM

A standout amongst the most energizing and remunerating parts of the real estate investing procedure happens when you really sell your property. Despite the fact that it tends to be anything but difficult to end up made up for lost time in the expectation of the nearby, it's critical to look after core interest. Similarly as in some other segment of this procedure, you should be speedy and productive. You realize that the quicker you sell, the more productive you are. The less time your property spends sitting available will set aside you cash in holding costs—just as valuable time that you ought to spend on your next venture. Now we have a completed rehab that is arranged with expert pictures that is prepared to market and sell!

Selling a property is a work of art. Before we dive into the subtleties of the framework, recollect that purchasing a house is commonly the greatest investment the normal American will make in their lifetime. To state that a purchaser is restless all through the home purchasing procedure is putting it mildly. Some portion of your job, in this manner, is to comforted the purchaser during the walkthrough so they're ready to rationally begin moving into the house without a moment's pause. I have sold completed rehabs that range in completed costs from $60,000 to $1,450,000, and higher. Following the selling framework I have spread out enables you to pitch to both top of the line and first-time homebuyer value focuses.

The main thing that feels more noteworthy than selling your property is preselling the property before you even put it available.

Preselling happens when you're ready to advance and sell a house before remodels are completely finished. You may accept that you would never sell a home in these condition— rundown, dividers half crushed, yard in grave condition. Be that as it may, this procedure gives purchasers a vested thought of how you're improving the property and how it will look when all is said and finished with your extent of work close by. The course of events I use to begin preselling my properties is around about fourteen days preceding posting the property on the

Multiple Listing Service (MLS). There are six battles that I've looked for some kind of employment best during the presale stage. A portion of these procedures can be viewed as guerrilla showcasing, which is a greater amount of an in-your-face style of getting things done; however at times that is the thing that you have to do around here.

House standards are an incredible method to publicize your home while it's as yet being rehabbed furthermore, they draw bunches of consideration and make an incredible buzz. Take a stab at utilizing things like "We Buy

Houses" scoundrel signs to put outside your property. Marauder signs are publicizing signs put out in obvious areas simply like political battles signs you see all through town during races.

Another choice is to make a sign with a connection to your blog or site so the neighbors can pursue your redesign's advancement. In addition to the fact that this helps you produce purchaser drives, it additionally tells your temporary workers that individuals are viewing—so they better keep things adequate while taking a shot at your task.

Neighbor referrals can be an enormous asset when selling your property. The general population who live nearest to this rehabbed property are regularly the home's best salesmen. One approach to connect with neighbors is to utilize "Pick Your Neighbor" flyers. You—or somebody in your office—make a flyer with your name, organization, logo, and a concise passage clarifying how individuals in the network ought to pick their next neighbor by alluding quality purchasers to you. You can likewise get neighbors required through entryway thumping, which is like cold pitching, yet ought to be more invited since you are endeavoring to rejuvenate the area. Ensure you contact around 5 to 10 nearby neighbors who are in strolling separation. Tell them your objective and possibly offer a reward for referrals. Show how energized you are about the property and welcome them to see it themselves at the open house. No one needs an awful neighbor, so local people love telling their loved ones who have appeared in moving into their neighborhood previously.

Content and telephone computerized hotlines are astounding approaches to discover purchasers. On the off chance that you publicize a telephone number on the facade of the house, you can advance your remodels and assemble a purchaser's rundown. You have a selection of administrations to make a commercial through a recorded message that depicts the home. At the point when a purchaser calls, you catch their telephone number, enabling you to get back to them.

We want to utilize a content cordial number that binds to our database. This enables invested individuals to content us to get posting and selling data and creates a recorded voice impact with subtleties of the property. We utilize a versatile promoting stage called Moby inside our database that enables us to use this astonishing bit of innovation.

Pocket-posting flyers to operators have constantly demonstrated to be an extraordinary promoting asset. Real estate specialists love having the option to see something that hasn't hit the market yet. Along these lines, when they meet with purchasers, they have a chance to demonstrate to them a property that nobody else approaches and hasn't hit the market yet.

Building a buyer list

You never need to be in a circumstance where you need to run around searching for purchasers. The best way to guarantee that doesn't occur is to have a quality purchasers list at your transfer. The greater and better the purchasers list, the quicker you will sell your property. The principle objective here is to ceaselessly develop the rundown of value purchasers, regardless of whether you don't have a property to sell at the time. This rundown ought to incorporate data like first and last name, email address, telephone number, purchasing criteria, kind of financing, and some other significant data. When you have your armory arranged and prepared to go, you need to keep up associations with each individual on that rundown and viably showcase your properties to them. Make sure to treat your rundown of purchasers like the gold mine it is.

Rehabbing isn't a property-focused business; it is a people-focused business. We purchase from individuals, pitch to individuals, and work with a wide range of individuals during the procedure to ensure things are done viably. Each spirit you experience should realize what you do and what administrations you offer. This is particularly evident when you are beginning to fabricate a purchasers list. Similarly as with any endeavor, concentrating without anyone else needs will never satisfy. You should endeavor your systems administration endeavors about the other individual. The law of correspondence will continually seem to be accurate. You will find that the more you accomplish for other people, the more they will need to accomplish for you.

At whatever point you meet anybody remotely keen on real estate of any sort, add the person in question to your purchasers list. That individual may not be prepared today, yet the person may very well call you up in three years. There are a few open doors that you should exploit when hoping to coordinate with potential purchasers—explicitly, organizing occasions.

Sending mass messages to everybody on your rundown builds your opportunity of increasing quality purchasers to add to your channel. You generally need to utilize an expert email communicate administration to do as such. Utilizing a database, for example, Realeflow will permit you the stage for legitimate email promoting. Another well known email advertising stage is Constant Contact. Making these strides will guarantee that you are looking after consistence, getting most extreme deliverability of your email, and remaining off of boycotts. Likewise incorporate a few connects to your sites and crush pages when you send these out. Email impacts ought to be reliably sent to different investors, real estate operators, contract merchants, and title specialists.

It is essential to successfully impart and pose the best possible inquiries when screening for your purchaser. While it is critical to meet with purchasers, it's increasingly essential to utilize a systemized way to deal with prescreening them. The fundamental two segments to concentrate on when examining these leads are money related readiness and mental arrangement. Monetarily, you need to ensure that the purchaser is working with and is qualified with a home loan agent or another monetary source to buy the home. On the off chance that the purchaser hasn't prearranged the financing, it is a marker that the person is just in the beginning periods of searching for a home.

On the off chance that the individual in question isn't working with a loan specialist, at that point you need to promptly put that individual in contact with your favored home loan agent. You would prefer not to sit around idly indicating homes that are out of the purchaser's value run or that they essentially are not monetarily qualified or prepared to purchase. On the off chance that you are working with a money purchaser, you will need to confirm a proof of assets. You won't ordinarily pitch to a money purchaser since you are selling completed retail rehab properties; be that as it may, it occurs every now and then.

Notwithstanding when somebody is monetarily set they up, may not be sincerely prepared. In the event that your potential purchaser hasn't done the exploration and the arrangement important to proceed with purchasing a home, they are likely not going to move. A ton of retail purchasers are in the beginning periods of searching for a property, and may not be prepared to purchase a property promptly, however they might be prepared sooner rather than later. That is the reason you should spare all prospect data in your database. Who the purchaser meets with will rely upon whether you have the house recorded. On the off chance that you list your property, at that point you will need your specialist to meet with the purchaser. In any case, on the off chance that you choose to offer it without the MLS, you should meet with the purchaser yourself. Remember that as your business develops, you can redistribute this undertaking to somebody in your office.

Listing your property

You were not ready to make any moves during the presale stage, the following stage is to list your property. You essential objective here is to increase most extreme presentation. The more purchasers you pull in, the almost certain it is that you will locate that one individual who cherishes and is able to purchase the property. It is evaluated that 97 percent of purchasers discover the house they need online before they even call the purchaser. Regardless of whether you utilize the MLS, syndicated postings, or both, getting your property recorded brings you one bit nearer to finding your purchaser. Pick the best Realtor who will execute the promoting efforts you require and get your completed rehab posting on the MLS. This site gets the most purchaser eyeballs of any selling stage. You'll need to make an agenda to enable you to plan for how you're going to sell this home. Archives, for example, the accompanying precedent will assist you with starting an establishment for advertising your properties the correct way.

A specialist can enable you to sell your home on the MLS at the most noteworthy value conceivable, help you consult during the procedure, and close on schedule while working with escrow or the lawyer. The truth of the matter is that rehab investors who comprehend the intensity of the association with a decent Realtor are the best investors in the business. The two gatherings can offer important administrations to one another, subsequent in organizations that work together for higher checks.

When you're prepared to begin your scan for the correct operators, make a point to get your work done and make a few inquiries among companions and associates, just as previous neighbors who may have sold in the previous year. This will be a long haul relationship, so it's well worth investing the additional energy in advance to coordinate with the best.

Operators ought to be solid, quick, and willing to gain proficiency with your real estate investing process. A decent specialist has an extraordinary system of purchasers and expert connections that you can take advantage of. It's essential to manufacture associations with specialists who have information in your area and who rundown in your general vicinity. Their experience showcasing inside that area can get a great deal of traffic. You can inquire about their history by taking a gander at the MLS to discover operators with the most deals.

Costing

Real estate deals commissions are part an assortment of ways. Generally, a real estate operator who records a property is paid a level of the home's selling cost, and the posting specialist will ordinarily offer generally 50% of that commission to the purchaser's specialist in the exchange. The normal expense and commission is between a 5 to 6 percent posting commission that is shared between a posting representative and a purchaser merchant for a standard posting. In the event that you ever choose not to utilize an operator on an arrangement, a few merchants do offer what is known as a level charge posting. In this situation, you consent to pay the purchaser's specialist and a little charge to a posting merchant, however not consenting to the full posting expense. A level expense financier will take the administrations customarily done by a specialist and rundown the property available to be purchased in the neighborhood MLS without requiring the vender to utilize administrations, for example, valuation help, arrangement, exchange the board, or appearing. As far as I can tell, a full-administration specialist is desirable over a level charge administration. On the off chance that your property does not sell, you are continually going to think about whether you ought to have gone with a full-administration Realtor as opposed to being modest on the posting commission. Keep in mind—you profit when you purchase; yet you realize your cash when you really sell the property.

At the point when the opportunity arrives to have an open house, the primary concern you should concentrate on is having the option to create parts and heaps of traffic. You need however much movement going on as could reasonably be expected to make the vitality you has to get things going. This can be an in all respects convenient and costeffective approach to acquaint your home with potential purchasers. The initial step is to settle on the date and time. Ends of the week, especially Sunday evenings, work best. Exploit when individuals are all over the place, searching for activities, and anticipating open houses. Check the logbook in your neighborhood ensures you aren't clashing with any enormous occasions occurring that day. You may even need to check with the nearby open works office to check whether any development will continue during the season of your open house that may cause temporary routes. The following stage is to showcase and promote your open house so as to get individuals in the entryway. Likewise with the majority of your showcasing endeavors, focus on what works and recollect that the easily overlooked details are what check.

Word of mouth

When you are making your open-house plans, have a lot of signs saying "Open House This Weekend" with inflatables around the area. These signs have been around for a long, long time and there's an explanation behind that—they work! This apparatus is a basic, lowtech, and reasonable type of showcasing that is amazingly powerful.

Ensure you put these signs out a couple of days before the occasion. In the event that you plan on having your open house on Sunday, attempt and get the signs out by Friday—and dependably incorporate the occasion's date and time. Most MLSs the nation over will enable you to post an open house and enable nearby real estate specialists to direct open house visits. A significant number of these operators will take their customers on these visits to abstain from losing them to another specialist. Use Craigslist, Zillow, Trulia, or other online arranged sites to make a viable advertisement that is simple for individuals to seek. Use watchwords in your advertisements to pull in your group; you need your property to be wherever your crowd is looking.

Online networking has turned out to be one of the greatest promoting outlets. By and by, on the off chance that you have a business page or potentially an individual page on Facebook, you need to share all the fervor of your open house with your system. When you tell your Facebook companions that you are selling a property, every one of them has the chance to impart that data to their companions, which will get the message out quickly. Making an occasion on Facebook for your open house is an incredible method to get extra web based life buzz and influence.

Neighbors frequently need to help pick the following purchaser that will be a piece of their locale and may know loved ones who need to move into the area. Advise them regarding how the home's selling cost will influence their property estimations. You can likewise utilize neighbor letters in the event that they aren't home so as to viably promote your property. People leasing a home in the region could likewise seize the chance to at long last claim.

A standout amongst the best post office based mail crusades includes mailing to tenants who have a 720 FICO rating or higher in the picked territories. In the event that you can, get a rundown of a leaseholders and get in touch with them about the home you have available to be purchased today, and the capacity to purchase later on. An open house is an incredible open door for you to convey email impacts to your purchasers rundown and fax impacts to other neighborhood real estate operators about your open house. At the point when realty workplaces have their morning gatherings, there is frequently a dialog of the movement in the region. In situations where stock is low and purchaser request is high, neighborhood open houses are probably going to be appeared at these gatherings.

While you are promoting for individuals to go to your open house, ensure that each corner of the property is prepared for the spotlight. As I underscored beforehand, organizing is a significant component when selling. A standard guideline for the expense of contracting an expert stager who has their very own furnishings and material is .5 to 1 percent of the posting cost of your home. Follow-up is basic. You need to continually endeavor to associate with your potential purchasers and ensure that you are dependably at the bleeding edge of their brains. The most significant advance is to development and check in with potential invested individuals. In the event that somebody called, visited, or messaged you about your particular property, catch up with each lead until your property is sold. No one can really tell where your purchaser is going to originate from, so be determined!

CHAPTER 13: POSTGAME ANALYSIS

Since you've sold your property, it's a great opportunity to make a stride back and investigate your arrangement. It's essential to do this toward the finish of every real estate exchange so you can make sense of what you did well and what you fouled up. It's dependably a smart thought to contrast your anticipated with your genuine benefit, and perceive where things worked and where they didn't. This will shield you from committing a similar error twice.

To be fantastic or uncommon at any control, you need to reliably move in the direction of acing your specialty. In the event that we simply work, work, work relentless while never taking one moment to dissect what we're doing, we'll never distinguish where we have to improve. By ceasing to audit what we're doing and where we are going, we keep on recognizing enhancements and efficiencies that will quicken our business. Above all, the time you take to survey a past arrangement will enable you to get more cash-flow on a future arrangement. Working without really breaking down on the off chance that we are, truth be told, improving keeps us from really showing signs of improvement and heading the correct way. It is significant that we as a whole set aside the effort to investigate and postgame our endeavors and gain from our great and terrible application. When we postgame appropriately we can enhance each extend we complete.

Each rehabber ought to do what I call a postgame examination after each undertaking. This method involves a successful bookkeeping framework and closeout process that can enable you to find each penny of your rehab benefits and costs. It will assist you with determining whether you effectively assessed rehab costs, holding times, and whether you made an enormous enough benefit. Frameworks are essential to your prosperity and won't be as powerful without legitimate principles. Standards are not hard to set; they're difficult to pursue. That is the reason each colleague you have and each worker you contract needs to purchase in toward the objectives in which you're working and the standards you've set. On the off chance that they don't, you will experience serious difficulties dealing with your group and improving efficiency.

Filing System Organization

Regardless of the amount you endeavor to do on the web and how hard you attempt to work a paperless business, you will definitely need to manage and remain over desk work. Notwithstanding whether you utilize a paper documenting framework or work electronically, it's imperative to build up an efficient framework. The manner in which we document and compose our archives enables us to be viable and gainful. Keeping your recording framework composed guarantees that everybody in your group can without much of a stretch sort out, distinguish, and discover data and archives when required. You ought to have two separate envelopes for every property: a month to month receipt organizer and an ace property envelope.

The month to month receipt organizer will have subfolders for solicitations, receipts for gas/oil, electric, water, sewer, first home loan, second home loan, contracts and solicitations, and building grants. The ace property organizer will incorporate both purchasing and selling envelopes, and ought to be kept in a bolted file organizer. This document contains private data, for example, purchasers' Social Security numbers or price tag. The entire thought is to rehab properties without doing practically everything yourself. So when you enlist or expedite your first colleague, this is a simple to follow framework for them to execute and take work off your plate. They just need to get to the recording and paying of the month to month charges in the month to month receipt organizer for your bookkeeping purposes. This framework takes into consideration development and takes you from expert to entrepreneur a great deal sooner and with a versatile framework to execute your bookkeeping and recording.

Post-rehab accounting

You won't discover numerous real estate investors feeling impatient when it comes time to do accounting and bookkeeping. Be that as it may, regardless of whether it isn't some tea, you should know about each watch that comes in and each look at that goes. I've seen numerous investors get exclusive focus taking a gander at their properties' buy costs, deal costs, and rehab costs. Too many overlook the regular dollar sums and exchanges engaged with utilities, financing charges, shutting expenses, and other holding costs. When you ask them how much benefit they made on a rehab bargain, they can't give you an answer!

There is no reason that you shouldn't realize each and every dollar spent or made on an arrangement down to the penny. The exact opposite thing you need to happen is to leave the end table reasoning that you made $30,000 when you really just made $10,000. You'll can't be sure if you're running a proficient, successful, productive business. More terrible, you may not know whether you're notwithstanding making a benefit. Your business' prosperity relies upon the benefit of each arrangement, so you must track every exchange down to the penny. Be that as it may, before you begin utilizing bookkeeping programming like QuickBooks, you'll have to comprehend the basics. The fundamental capacity of a bookkeeping framework is just sorting out budgetary data and giving precise reports to follow your cash. You don't need to be a specialist, yet you ought to get comfortable with bookkeeping standards and strategies. Having a working information of bookkeeping before you hand it off to a clerk enables you to finish your very own governing rules too.

Quickbooks

Generally, you can execute your bookkeeping all around just with QuickBooks. QuickBooks Pro or QuickBooks Online are anything but difficult to-utilize bookkeeping projects intended to push little to medium-sized organizations know precisely where they stand monetarily and how to be progressively powerful. The apparatuses monitor client and merchant data by means of checks, keeps point by point data for every single financial balance in the business, and enable you to run reports. They additionally deal with any stock you have (the properties you purchase and sell). While there is surely more than one approach to set up and do your representing a rehab and flip business, I will share the framework I've utilized for as long as decade for following and finishing off a large number of properties. So as to keep a precise record of your assets and where your organization stands monetarily, you'll need accounting and bookkeeping frameworks that are set up for the whole deal and that can support development. There are various sorts of bookkeeping programming accessible; I like to work with and observe QuickBooks to be extremely basic and direct.

Income statement

The income statement, or benefit and misfortune explanation, abridges your organization's incomes and costs over some undefined time frame. Numerous organizations take a gander at a quarterly or yearly P&L to see their exhibition and perceive whether they are really profiting. Such huge numbers of real estate investors are unfit to address that question on seven days to week, month to month, or even a quarterly premise. A P&L with appropriate detailing will enable you to do only that by following your items' benefit by means of the incomes and expenses related with the item (specifically, the house). As a result of the kind of item you're selling, your P&L will indicate huge spikes each four to a half year when you sell a completed rehab and get a $30,000 to $60,000 rehab benefit.

The expenses in regards to the buy of a property will shift and incorporate the sum we buy the property for and the end expenses related with that exchange. These expenses are altogether promoted and put in our advantage account inside our bookkeeping framework. You would set up a benefit account (we utilized fixed resource for this reason) in your graph of records with the property address. You'll likewise build up a risk or credit account in the diagram of records with the property address. You should record any obtained assets (regardless of whether new credit or accepted home loan) as an obligation.

Rehab expenses are every one of the expenses related with materials and work during the rehab. Rehab costs likewise incorporate all holding expenses. Basically, the rehab expenses incorporate anything spent to remodel the property that will remain with the property. When you spend this cash, you record it in the advantage account you set up when the property was obtained. The rehab assets increment the complete estimation of the benefit record and basically add to the cost premise of your unique buy and securing cost and cost. Conveying expenses are those expenses acquired to hold the property. These incorporate any home loan or advance installments for the property, property charges, protection premiums, utility installments (water, power, gas, rubbish, and so on.), garden care (once the rehab is finished, etc.

Selling expenses are the expenses caused so as to get the property sold commissions, any end costs paid in the interest of the purchaser, selling shutting costs, any home loan or advance adjustments, etc. This classification additionally incorporates things the purchaser has required as a component of the buy contract. For instance, if the purchaser needs you to put a fence around the property so as to close, at that point you could represent that as a feature of the selling costs. In any case, if the purchaser requires a particular fix that ought to have been made as a piece of the rehab procedure, I would incorporate it in the rehab costs. The deal is the point at which we enter a diary section to discount the all out equalizations in the advantage and risk records to record the expense of offers and the returns got as income. This section enables the program to compute your addition or misfortune, which is appeared on the salary proclamation. For example, suppose you buy a property for $100,000 and offer it for $180,000 after rehab. The benefit would be $80,000 less the expenses brought about in obtaining, conveying, and selling the property.

Building a team

Leverage is the way to accomplishing progressively, developing more, and procuring more. You don't really need to enlist representatives so as to fabricate an incredible real estate group when first beginning. It is basic to see, nonetheless, that enlisting or paying self-employed entities to maintain certain regions of your business can result in more arrangements and get more benefit.

You need your group of experts to incorporate a selling real estate operator, a real estate exchange lawyer or escrow organization (contingent upon the state in which you work, you should make it all work out with lawyers or escrow organizations), a home loan facilitate, a property supervisor, a protection specialist and protection expedite, a hard-cash and private moneylender, and a title organization. These experts get remuneration because of each gainful arrangement. These key connections will make you progressively effective, enable you to move quicker, and get more cash when you set aside the effort to prescreen, meet, and select the best. There are likewise a couple of other individuals you'll need to expedite board to enable your group to work as flawlessly as would be prudent.

Your first contract ought to be an associate who can assist you with promoting, take leads, investigate arrangements, and complete undertakings like running errands and carrying out some regulatory responsibilities. Basically, your first contract must be a cooperative person who will remove work from your work area and give you an opportunity to gain more arrangements. The second individual you should contract is an acquisitions and showcasing director. This current person's significant need will be to concentrate on actualizing promoting and recognizing arrangements to put under contract. Your third contract should be a rehab venture chief who pursues the rehab frameworks clarified in this book, and keeps on finding and oversee quality contractual workers while finishing rehab ventures. The fourth individual you should contract is the liquidation and deals showcasing director, whose principle employment ought to be centered around selling the majority of your rehabs and discount bargains. In the event that you would preferably not have this situation in-house, enlisting an A+ posting specialist in your group can fill it.

At the point when your business begins to develop, your time is best spent finding arrangements, cash, or purchasers. In the long run, as your business turns out to be increasingly computerized, you need to have the option to enlist quality ability into your organization, deal with those people, and persuade them to achieve extraordinary things inside your association. That is the place re-appropriating becomes possibly the most important factor. Each effective business at last turns into a people business—so the better you become at discovering, rousing, preparing, and overseeing quality individuals, the more fruitful your business will turn into. The objective of redistributing to colleagues, representatives, or specialist organizations is to delegate work that must be done all together for the business to look after itself. In the event that you have frameworks set up and set up a skillful group, you are as of now in an ideal position to re-appropriate most of your indispensable day by day exercises.

The most significant errand you have is to execute frameworks and give a structure where other individuals can prevail in your business. At the point when other colleagues, workers, or self employed entities have accomplishment in your business framework, you will have additional time back in your life. The hardest activity is to flame yourself from an errand and hand it off to another colleague. Practice this procedure and do it more than once. In the long run you will fire yourself out of the considerable number of occupations in your business so you can really have a business that works for you rather than you working for it.

CHAPTER 14: COMMON SELLING BUSINESS

The greatest mistake an investor can make is to not gain from other investors' mix-ups. I was so siphoned about my first rehab venture when I initially began—so energized that You should, obviously, be amped up for what you do, yet don't give that fervor a chance to shield you from avoiding potential risk and fundamental strides to have an effective undertaking. An excessive number of investors think back on their first tasks and kick themselves for succumbing to a portion of the senseless oversights I determine in this section. Basic stumbles, for example, introducing machines before the house is finished, putting in ground surface before all the tradesman have completed, or just not having a week by week house checkup framework in the winter to guarantee the channels don't stop would all be able to signify gigantic cerebral pains. A portion of the things I have taken in the most difficult way possible will enable you to abstain from stalling out with a property… or far more atrocious, having your very own bad dream story to tell.

Leaving the property unsecured

Security is a top need. Since your hands are not by any means the only ones on the undertaking, you'll need to avoid potential risk. We as a whole need to trust that everybody we work with and the area is dependable and safe; in any case, in some cases it's simply not the situation. Leaving a property unbound is an oversight you would prefer not to make. Changing the lockbox code, utilizing floodlights, and turning a radio on in the nighttimes are only a couple of the manners in which you can stop hoodlums who are searching for a simple score. No one can tell who still has a lot of keys when you first buy a property or what contractual worker will return with the current lockbox code. Change the locks from the very first moment and put a lockbox on the entryway so that tradesmen can travel every which way unreservedly. As you close culmination, you'll have an ever increasing number of completed materials and assets in the house that you have to verify and secure.

When the woodworker, handyman, circuit tester, and HVAC have introduced their installations and the redesign has been finished, change the lockbox code again with the goal that solitary the offering group approaches the house. This decreases the quantity of individuals going in and out who could wander off with any resources in the property.

When you begin your task and absolutely when you complete, a standout amongst the best burglary avoidance frameworks you can utilize is lighting. I realize it sounds straightforward, however you'd be astounded—many individuals simply don't consider it. Put sunset to-day break floodlights at the back and front of your property. When it gets dull, that property will be lit up like Yankee Stadium. I likewise prefer to keep a couple of the lights on in the house also. Regularly, we'll place the lights in different rooms all through and set up clocks on them. Doing as such makes it vague to individuals in the area whether the property is really empty or not. We need bystanders to address on the off chance that somebody is really living on the property.

One of the more clear approaches to avoid robbery is by introducing an alert framework. It doesn't need to be best in class; you can generally introduce a versatile caution framework. There are moderate, basic costs offered on frameworks that can give month to month observing. On the off chance that you need a significantly progressively moderate choice, you can likewise show little signs in the window or in the front garden just to give the appearance that caution frameworks are set up.

Skimping on landscaping

Finishing is the most significant purpose of contact with a client searching for another home. The front of the house is your publicizing publication for the property, so why not approach it with as much consideration and consideration as you do with the remainder of the rehab? You ought to dependably have your leave system in the cutting edge of your psyche, and be considering how you can improve your odds of selling your property. Arranging is only one case of a reasonable yet viable unfortunate obligation—which is the reason it ought to be one of the principal things on your motivation. You don't need to transform the front yard of your property into a professional flowerbed; be that as it may, it is stunning to perceive what a pleasant, cut garden, several bushes, and a couple of complement blossoms can do to a property's appearance and attractiveness. Realize that the outside of a house says a lot about within, and about the proprietor. Deal with the seemingly insignificant details and ensure that you improve your home's entrance and make guests feel welcome. Neglecting to exhibit a wow factor outwardly keeps potential purchasers from strolling in the entryway. Great finishing can truly change your home's outside look and feel. Contract a gardener to carry out the responsibility expertly, and perceive how the outcomes get individuals.

Maintaining property

This next mistake is a particularly basic one to stay away from. You can finish the best venture of your life, yet on the off chance that you don't deal with the property, you will experience serious difficulties offering it. An absence of upkeep before all else will make you miss the most significant flood of purchasers.

Keeping up on the control offer is similarly as significant as making it. So regardless of whether you worked superbly on arranging, recollect that grass develops and brambles will dependably need cutting. It is anything but an assignment that you can do once, clear the soil off your hands, and proceed onward.

Except if you sell the property rapidly, you'll need to remain over upkeep. On the off chance that your property is in a bad way all things considered, at that point it won't resemble an expert is dealing with it.

Try not to be the just one stressed over how your task looks. Your whole group should have a similar want to dependably be on their A game. An apathetic outside mirrors a lethargic inside and that is not the picture that you need your purchasers to have about the house you're selling. Make your desires obvious to your contractual workers in advance. Despite the fact that this is delineated in your temporary worker records, advise them that you are continually searching for more tasks and on the off chance that they need to keep on getting business from you, they need to tidy up their wreckage and keep the house looking incredible.

CHAPTER 15: A SYSTEM FOR KEEPING AND GROWING BUSINESS

The main thing that gets me more energized than rehabbing real estate is developing and dealing with the cash we make from rehabbing real estate. Individuals who have more cash are utilizing a greater amount of the expense code to spare and keep a greater amount of their cash. The data contained in this book isn't just about how you to get more cash-flow, yet to keep the cash that you make. Picking and recognizing an element to work together is a significant choice. You can purchase and sell real estate as a sole owner, obviously. Notwithstanding, when you do volume and different exchanges, there are a great deal of advantages to setting up an appropriate element and assetprotection plan within the near future.

There are more determinations accessible for shaping a business element; in any case, these are the three substances that are regularly utilized and concentrated on. Take some time and research these with your ideal expert to distinguish the best fit for your own and money related circumstance. We give our understudies the experts, the assets, and the group to duplicate our structure that we use so they can recreate our fruitful structure and push ahead.

My main responsibility is to walk you through the data you have to expand your budgetary education. This will enable you to invest more energy with your particular expert to settle on the best choice dependent on your own and money related objectives. One specific territory of guidance that is urgent to cover is the manner by which to hold and possess long haul resources, for example, investment properties.

It isn't savvy from a risk point of view to possess your long haul resources in a similar substance you use to rehab and discount properties. On the off chance that you get sued—which ideally won't occur, however may—and have every one of your advantages in a single element, at that point those benefits are liable to the case of the claim. This is the thing that makes this partition so basic.

Money Allocation Strategies

Individuals often ask me how we ought to dispense the benefits we make from our arrangements. A standard guideline that I show my understudies how to represent your charges, business investments, and individual use is to consider taking the benefits you make from a rehab and allotting them into six unique cans for appropriate arranging and development.

You will see that first pail, charges, is the biggest. I exhort apportioning benefits from your ongoing arrangements into it. By executing a portion of the techniques I share, you will most likely diminish a decent bit of your assessable salary. The second pail, development capital—which includes your very own investment into your scholarly resources and different apparatuses and frameworks to use for your business—is the most significant investment you can make. Similarly as you put resources into this book, you can take one thought and framework I partook in this book and make multiple times the investment in real estate benefit. The third pail goes legitimately back to your business to keep it developing and thriving through showcasing dollars and overhead needs. You won't probably keep rehabbing except if you have persuaded openings (bargains) that your promoting dollars and exercises have gotten. As you assemble and develop your business, you will have certain hazard and business situations against which you will need to protect. The customary protection market does not give protection to each hazard that entrepreneurs bring about. Hostage protection is an option in contrast to this situation. A hostage is an insurance agency framed to cover the dangers of its parent organization. Premiums that the parent working organization pays to an appropriately organized hostage for property and setback inclusion should be charge deductible to the parent organization.

In this situation, an enterprise or element with at least one backups sets up a hostage insurance agency as a claimed auxiliary. The hostage is promoted and domiciled in a purview with hostage empowering enactment that enables the hostage to work as an authorized safety net provider. The parent recognizes the dangers of its auxiliaries that it needs the hostage to endorse. The hostage assesses the dangers, composes approaches, sets premium dimensions, and acknowledges premium installments. The backups at that point make good on the hostage regulatory obligation deductible premium installments. At that point the hostage, similar to any safety net provider, contributes the top notch installments for future case payouts. At the point when the time of the in danger premium is finished, the insurance agency would now be able to hold the premium for its own utilization. At the point when done the right way, you could set up and possess a hostage that your real estate investment business pays premiums to for certain business dangers. When the top notch year closes—and if in actuality your real estate organization did not make a case on the protection—at that point your hostage organization can contribute and coordinate that premium for its very own advantage. The key here is you possess the real estate investment organization that gets the protection advantage just as the cost of doing business of the yearly premium. Furthermore, you possess the insurance agency that gets the opportunity to hold the premium after the safeguarded year in danger.

CONCLUSION

In the event that every single one of us seeks after our objectives in real estate, we can aggregately have a momentous social effect. Rehabbing houses is a very ground-breaking approach to accomplish a standout amongst the most critical human drivers: the need to contribute. Our responsibility to bettering homes leads a long ways past a fixed establishment and new windows. Consider it. Each time we take on another rehab, we are making another home for a purchaser to accomplish their fantasy of home possession to make deep rooted recollections in. We are improving neighborhoods, expelling cursed, appalling houses, and expanding the estimation of adjacent homes. We are making occupations for every one of the general population we contract to chip away at the home, adding income to our city and town by pulling grants, and animating the economy with the buy of each new bureau and material we put into our completed rehabs.

On a more fabulous scale, we make benefits that enable us to utilize our assets for more noteworthy's benefit. Being a fruitful investor gives us additional time, vitality, and cash that we can use to give back. I have found that new investors and business visionaries, who offer a pledge to decidedly adding to their general surroundings, dependably have better, all the more suffering achievement in their business. They are consistently searching for approaches to give back, bolster foundations, and compassionate endeavors.

Individuals frequently ask me for what good reason I mentor and show real estate as opposed to concentrating on discovering more arrangements for myself. The most fulfilling and satisfying procedure I can have is helping another investor make progress through shared learning, frameworks, and experience. Be that as it may, considerably more remunerating than that is to see those equivalent investors seek after a higher reason and a show preemptive kindness attitude, appearing by helping other people.

Forgetting about outdoor

Outside lighting isn't something you may consider immediately when starting your rehab; in any case, everything adds to the significant initial introduction. An awful early introduction might be the main thing a potential purchaser needs to abstain from taking a gander at a property through and through. Give a purchaser who chooses to drive by around evening time something to get amped up for. Night is the most emotional time to see your finishing. On the off chance that appropriately lit, homes can emit an extremely warm and welcoming feel. Lighting apparatuses likewise impart an improved suspicion that all is well and good. Their quality additionally enlightens attributes that you wish to show, further adding to the general feel of the property. Whenever executed to the potential purchaser's enjoying, they will need to inundate themselves in the home's highlights much further.

Another extraordinary alternative is to utilize sun powered lighting, which is an astounding decision for adding a delicate feel to the front of the house without utilizing any vitality other than the sun. You unquestionably must be cautious where you place these lights, since they may not be helpful if your front yard has an excessive amount of shade. When introducing sunlight based lighting, use spotlights that have an assortment of settings to figure out where the light would look best. You additionally need to check for whether you will sparkle light into your neighbor's home.

You should go well beyond the nature of the contenders item that you are placing out into the commercial center. You need to recall that for a homebuyer, picking a spot to live is, to an enormous degree, a passionate undertaking. It is tied in with finding that exceptional spot that feels perfectly in the wake of a monotonous day of work, school, an excursion for work, or where one securely raises a family. Regularly, a property neglects to sell since it doesn't have anything extraordinary to isolate it from the challenge. Those hoping to improve the highlights of their home would be more qualified to concentrate on explicit rooms. As a large portion of you know, kitchens and washrooms are the basic rooms that at last assistance a house to sell, so investing your time and cash principally into those rooms will yield you the best outcomes. Imminent homebuyers are normally attracted to these utilitarian regions, particularly the main washroom.

CPSIA information can be obtained
at www.ICGtesting.com
Printed in the USA
BVHW041150030919
557441BV00012B/115/P